101

Spiritual Lessons for Coaches and Athletes

Rodney Gaines, Ph.D.

Scripture taken from:

- The Holy Bible, NEW INTERNATIONAL VERSION®. © 1973, 1978, 1984 Biblica. All rights reserved throughout the world. Used by permission of Biblica.
- The New King James Version®. © 1982 by Thomas Nelson, Inc. Used by permission. All rights reserved.
- New Revised Standard Version Bible, © 1989 National Council of the Churches of Christ in the United States of America. Used by permission. All rights reserved.

ISBN: 978-1-60679-079-3
Library of Congress Control Number: 2009944030

Book layout: Bean Creek Studio
Cover design: Brenden Murphy
Text photos: ©2009 JupiterImages Corporation
Front cover photo: ©2009 JupiterImages Corporation

Coaches Choice
P.O. Box 1828
Monterey, CA 93942
www.coacheschoice.com

Dedication

I would first like to dedicate this book to God, who gave me the mind and ability to write the many stories in this book from reading His word. I also dedicate this book to my parents, Randolph and Emma Gaines. And to my brother, Wayne, and three sisters, Glenda, Darlene, and Sharon. I also would like to thank my cousin Robert Tompkins for all of the Bible studies we had over the phone from a distance. I also dedicate this book to many friends, coaches, and athletes, and pray that this book will give them a stronger relationship with God and a better walk in life.

Acknowledgments

I would first like to acknowledge God for giving me the ability to complete this project. I also would like to acknowledge James Peterson at Coaches Choice for giving me the opportunity to write and would like to thank him for his encouragement. I also would like to thank Kristi Huelsing for her patience and for helping me through the edits of the book. And I would like to acknowledge the following friends, who gave me encouragement to write: Oliver Washington, Steve Upton, Dr. Delano Tucker, Mrs. Paula Shaw, Dr. Linda Person, Dr. Becky Nelson, Dr. Kerry Redican, Dr. Richard Stratton, Pamela Nicholas, Lindsey Humphries, Eric Viets, Terrence Brand, and Wardell Nottingham. I would also like to thank my pastor Bishop Courtney McBath in Norfolk, VA, Dr. John Maxwell, Dr. Samuel Chand, Bishop T.D. Jakes, and Dr. Kenneth Ulmer for their teachings and ministry. Finally, I would like to acknowledge the many coaches around the United States who encouraged me to write, and who said that their life was positively affected by the weekly newsletters that God allowed me to write.

Contents

1

Success

#1: God's Promise for Success

For surely I know the plans I have for you, says the Lord, plans for
your welfare and not for harm, to give you a future with hope.
Then when you call upon me and come and pray to me,
I will hear you.
                                        —Jeremiah 29:11-12

God already has a vision for our life and He lets us know that He is going to prosper us. God knows how many strands of hair each of us have on our head. In order to be successful, we must line up with God's vision for our life. So many times, we lose sight of our goals and dreams, because we forget what God has said. He has already declared that he will prosper us, and make a way for us to succeed.

Our superiors can oftentimes see things that we can't see. They are looking through a different set of spectacles, and they are spectacles of experience. It is important that we seek wise counsel from our superiors. As we have often heard, we can't put all our trust in man or woman, because people hurt us. God always prospers us, and we can trust our life in His hands. He declares that we will have a future. If we are going to have a future, this promise means success. If we live to see another day, it is a success in itself.

In order for God to do His part, He is waiting to see if we are going to do our part. Every person must seek God through prayer and reading the word of God, the Holy Bible. It is our roadmap to success in any sport, position, or situation. In order to reach the success level God has planned for us, we have to call on His name, and we have to pray. Our prayers are heard by God, and in Jeremiah 29:11 God tells us that He will listen to our request.

Sometimes, an athlete does not give it her all. Perhaps, she is saving her energy for the end of the ball game. In order to win, God is telling us that we must seek Him with all of our heart. We can't run at half pace, and we can't give 90 percent. In Jeremiah 29:12, God tells us first to seek, so we must be listening for His voice, and then we must wholeheartedly seek Him with all of our heart and mind. No malingering can exist when it comes to seeking God.

We should renew our vision. We already know that we are going to be successful, because God declares it in His word. Some steps must be taken in order to succeed as a team or as an individual. We must trust God's vision for our life, and know that no matter what the outcome, God has already declared victory in our life. We have a hedge of protection over us as we strive for what God has laid up ahead for us. In order to prosper, we must come to God, and pray with all of our heart.

#2: The Bridge to Success

Jesus said to him, "I am the way, and the truth, and the life.
No one comes to the Father except through me."
—John 14:6

Usually, when a promise is made, some things exist on our end that we must uphold to receive that promise. A coach may tell his team that they are going to have a great feast if each player gives it her all during practice. Even with this promise, some players may not obey or accept the will of the coach. They may say, "I will receive the feast even if I just go through the motions," which is the mentality of today's world. They will just go along for the ride, and they don't do the most important thing that God has asked them to do.

In John 14:6, Jesus states, "I am the way and the truth and the life. No one comes to the Father except through me." This statement is one of the most important declarations in the Bible. In order to have access to God's promise, we have to have Jesus as our Lord and Savior. We have to first have a relationship with Jesus Christ, and we have to repent or turn away from our sins and ask God for forgiveness for things of the past. Jesus tells us the way to success is through Him.

First, Jesus tells us, "I am the way." In order for each person on the team to succeed, they must follow the leadership of Jesus. Through believing in Him, we have direct access to God today and for eternal life. Everyone wants to know the way to success, and Jesus makes it clear that if we want to see God someday, we must go through Him. He is the center of everything, and He is our chief official.

Next, Jesus states that He is the truth. In John 1:14, He states, "And the Word became flesh and lived among us, and we have seen his glory, the glory as of a father's only son, full of grace and truth."

That statement says it all. Jesus came and lived with us for a little while, and showed us the way to serve and have a true relationship with God. He told us how to have access to God. Just as the coach doesn't have to give a hot meal to his players, God didn't have to give us Jesus. It is through the grace of God that we received this promise.

We all have hope of one day having a better life than the one on this earth. Jesus next tells us that He is life. Most people are not afraid of dying, but they are afraid that possibly they never lived. Many live this life, and as they get older they want another life that is better. That better life is through Jesus, which gives us eternal life with God.

In John 14:6, we learned that Jesus is the way, the truth, and the life. No one comes to God without following Jesus. We should follow Jesus' path and his beliefs, and pattern our lives after the Son of God.

#3: Finding Success Through Service

For those who want to save their life will lose it, and those who lose their life for my sake, and for the sake of the gospel, will save it.
—Mark 8:35

Just as the Son of Man came not to be served but to serve, and to give his life as a ransom for many.
—Matthew 20:28

Success is sometimes defined as acquiring wealth, having a certain job, living in a big house, and being praised in your hometown. In sports, success may be defined as leading the league in a certain statistic, scoring the winning basket, or running for the game-winning touchdown. Team success may be defined as winning a championship or major tournament. How does God define success? Success only comes when we give up ourselves for the team. We have to take one for the team.

If every player on a team has a servant heart, that team is going to be hard to beat. It starts with the leaders of the team. They must serve the rest of the team, and they must give up and sacrifice self for success. As the players give to the team, the team will in turn give to them. In order to gain success, we must give it away. God is clearly telling us in Mark 8:35 that it starts first with Him. We have to be on His team, and we must first die of self and get on God's team. In order for a seed to grow, it must fall to the ground and die. Afterwards, that seed will grow.

If this attitude becomes contagious in the locker room, we can have an atmosphere for success. If each person on the team starts laying his goals down and helps the others, then a team is bound for success. In Mark 8:35, Jesus is clearly telling us to give up self and life for Him, which is the way to first place and success. In order to be first, we must be last. Many times, athletes and coaches have a me-centered attitude ("The team has to play hard for me" or "My job is to get them to play hard"). But it is the other way around. It is each individual's job to play or coach hard for the team.

God also tells us that we have to lose our life for Him and the gospel. The gospel is living out the truth of God, and we learned that Jesus is the truth. No one comes to God unless they go through the Son. God's word is the gospel. It is the living truth of today, and we must follow God's word. In Romans 10:9-10, Jesus states, ""Because if you confess with your lips that Jesus is Lord and believe in your heart that God raised him from the dead, you will be saved. For one believes with the heart and so is justified, and one confesses with the mouth and so is saved. We just need to confess with our mouth that Jesus is Lord, and make Him first in our heart. The word tells us that we must also be justified and believe in our heart. If we confess with our mouth that Jesus is Lord, and give our heart to God, we will enjoy success here today and until we go to be with the Lord. This confession must be given to the team. As we live a life of servanthood and start serving others on our team, this attitude becomes contagious. Everyone on the team will want what we have. People will start to follow our way as we follow Jesus' way. This way is the mark of service; this way is following the gospel; and this way is the heart of a champion.

#4: Successes After Failure

*It happened, late one afternoon, when David rose from his couch
and was walking about on the roof of the king's house, that he
saw from the roof a woman bathing; the woman was very
beautiful. David sent someone to inquire about the woman. It was
reported, "This is Bathsheba daughter of Eliam, the wife of Uriah
the Hittite." So David sent messengers to get her, and she came to
him, and he lay with her. (Now she was purifying herself after her
period.) Then she returned to her house. The woman conceived;
and she sent and told David, "I am pregnant."*
—2 Samuel 11:2-5

Sometimes, the only way to learn is to have a train wreck. Everyone is bound to fail at some point at some phase in their life. We oftentimes fail to be on time, fail in finances, fail in relationships, have an injury of a muscle or joint, lose a job, or fail in grades. A new day always comes, and some of the best learning lessons come when we don't get what we want.

God promises us success, although many times we will fall short and fail at the game of life. What do we do when we fall short of our goals or we fail? We can look at the life of King David who failed, but was known as a man after God's own heart. David failed several times as the king, but was still honored by God. David still experienced success even after he failed. The key is to learn from our failures, and try not to move on too quickly after we fall. We have to get up as slow as the Lord wants us to, and although it may be painful, we have to rely on God's time of healing and recuperation. The same King David who defeated Goliath and who was later crowned as the King of Israel fell into hardship. He committed several sins, which included adultery, murder, and disobeying God by taking the census.

The verse at the beginning of this lesson shows that David failed big time when he slept with a married woman and committed adultery. He also later had her husband Uriah killed by having him placed on the frontline during battle. As a result, his one sin escalated to another sin. Nathan, the Prophet, called David out on his sin, and David took his sins to God.

Psalm 51:1 quotes a sinner's prayer for pardon: "Have mercy on me, O God; according to your steadfast love; according to your abundant mercy; blot out my transgressions."

Like David, we need to first confess our sins to God, and He will give us a clean heart like David. We also have the blood of Jesus, which covers all our sins. He still was recognized as a man after God's own heart. Like David in Philippians 3:13-14, we must forget what lies behind and reach forward to what lies ahead.

#5: A Successful Prayer

Jabez was honored more than his brothers, and his mother named him Jabez, saying, "Because I bore him in pain." Jabez called on the God of Israel, saying, "Oh that you would bless and enlarge my border, and that your hand might be with me, and that you would keep me from hurt and harm!" And God granted what he asked.
—1 Chronicle 4:9-10

Prayer is definitely a way of letting God know that we want a relationship with Him. Although Jabez was named pain by his mother, he chose to do something about it. He was not going to live out the stigma that had been placed on him. Many times, we are known by our name or our association from the past. Like Jabez, we have to ask God for favor. The Bible says that Jabez first called out to God and asked God to bless him. Perhaps his life was headed for heartbreak and troubled times, but Jabez chose to call out to God. God has mercy on us, and His word says that we receive not because we ask not. In Matthew 7:7-8, Jesus states, "Ask, and it will be given you; search, and you will find; knock, and the door will be open for you." For everyone who asks receives, and everyone who searches finds, and for everyone who knocks, the door will be opened.

Jabez had to ask God for the blessing in the same way we have to have faith and ask God for the blessing. But we must not doubt when we ask. Jabez meant what he prayed, and he received from God what he prayed for.

If any of you are lacking in wisdom, ask God, who gives to all generously and ungrudgingly, and it will be given you. But ask in faith, never doubting, for the one who doubts is like a wave of the sea, driven and tossed by the wind; for the doubter being double-minded and unstable in every way, must not expect to receive anything from the Lord.
—James 1:5-7

Next, Jabez asked for God to enlarge his borders, and God did it. Like Jabez, our borders will be enlarged with faith in Jesus Christ. We all have different dreams and aspirations, but if God wants us to be a pro athlete, win a certain tournament, or acquire a certain skill or education, He can and will do it. By reading His word and praying, God keeps his hands on us just like Jabez. He also protects us from the enemy. In Psalm 23:4, he prays, "Even though I walk through the darkest valley, I fear no evil; for you are with me. Your rod and your staff, they comfort me."

We have to pray like Jabez. We will be blessed, our borders will be expanded, God's hand of favor will be upon us, we will be protected in the valley, and God will answer our prayers.

#6: Success Through Perseverance

*David said to the Philistine, "You come against me with sword
and spear and javelin, but I come against you in the name of
the Lord Almighty, the God of the armies of Israel, whom you
have defied. This day the Lord will hand you over to me, and I'll
strike you down and cut off your head. Today, I will give the
carcasses of the Philistine army to the birds of the air and the
beasts of the earth, and the whole world will know that there is
a God in Israel. All those gathered here will know that it is not
by sword or spear that the Lord saves; for the battle is the
Lord's, and he will give all of you into our hands."*
—1 Samuel 17:45-47

As coaches and athletes, we are faced with huge hurdles and obstacles. Oftentimes, the opposition seems invincible, and we move forward in despair. In 1987, I witnessed my first Mr. Virginia Bodybuilding Championship, and oh, how I marveled at the size and talent of the other bodybuilders. Little did I know at that time that most of them were on steroids. Without knowing this fact, I trained rigorously to match up with these giants, thinking my hard efforts would eventually give me the same muscle. I competed in my first Mr. Virginia contest in 1991, placing third in the middleweights. I placed second in 1992 and 1993. "You are just too small," they said. "You don't have the total package to win the overall title." In 1995, I trained a whole year for the contest, losing 40 lbs. for the event. I did two competitions before the 1995 Mr. Virgina, and lost to a couple guys who were also getting ready for the big one. I began running the Virginia Tech football stadium to add mass and cuts to my quads, and one day a strong vision came over me. I saw myself winning the contest, and, being scared, I wept because it was so strong a vision. Two weeks later, I drove to Hampton, VA, after finishing my exams, and I won the middleweights, and went on that night to win the overall title of 1995 Mr. Virginia. The guy in my division outweighed me by 20 lbs., and I defeated him. The heavyweight winner was 220 lbs., the middleweight winner 195 lbs., and I was 170 lbs. I thank God all the time for this blessing. He is a good God, and he deserves all the glory.

God will help us overcome any mountain. We just have to believe and have faith. We must also do His will daily. I talked about how David ran to Goliath. Goliath stood nine feet tall, but David ran to him with no fear. We must have this faith with earthly troubles. Pray about your troubles and know that God will help you overcome them.

As the Philistine moved closer to attack him, David ran quickly toward the battle line to meet him, reaching into his bag and taking out a stone, he slung it and struck the Philistine on the forehead. The stone sank into his forehead, and he fell face down on the ground. So David triumphed over the Philistine with a sling and a stone; without a sword in his hand, he struck down the Philistine and killed him.

David ran and stood over him. He took hold of the Philistine's sword and drew it from the scabbard. After he killed him, he cut off his head with the sword. When the Philistines saw that their hero was dead, they turned and ran.

We should stay disciplined as Christians, and defeat all the Goliaths in our lives.

#7: Successful Thinking

Finally, beloved, whatever is true, whatever is honorable, whatever is just, whatever is pure, whatever is pleasing, whatever is commendable, if there is any excellence, and there is anything worthy of praise, think about these things.
—Philippians 4:8

This way of thinking may be the most neglected skill of all. As the Little Engine That Could in the children's book doubted his ability to climb over the mountain, so do we cast doubt on our abilities. The engine started off saying, "I think I can, I think I can." Until the engine believed in its heart that it could scale the challenging mountain, it remained the Little Engine That Could. As the engine got closer to the top of the mountain, it gained confidence and started saying, "I know I can, I know I can." We can go a step further. We can start out thinking positive from the start, and use positive thinking. Every step that we gain towards our goal should prompt us to say, "I know I can."

In Philippians 4:8, Paul starts out by saying "finally." Finally means that we have arrived at an important and crucial point in our goal or journey. We have reached a new height. He concludes this verse by saying, "think on these things." The first thing that Paul advises us to think on is whatever is true. We are creatures of what occupies our thoughts, and our thoughts lead to our actions. We must first think on the truth, and the truth will set us free. Psalm 25:4-5 states, "Make me to know your ways, O Lord; teach me your paths. Lead me in your truth, and teach me, for you are the God of my salvation; for you I wait all day long." We are lead by the truth of God, and His word is the truth. We need to follow everything the Lord has instructed us to do in His word.

We must also do what is honorable in the eyes of the Lord. One thing that honors the Lord is controlling our body. 1 Thessalonians 4:3-5 states, "For this is the will of God, your sanctification: that you abstain from fornication; that each one of you know how to control your own body in holiness and honor, not with lustful passion, like the gentiles who do not know God." By staying away from sins of the flesh, we bring honor to God. Proverbs 21:15 reads, "When justice is done, it is a joy to the righteous, but dismay to evildoers." Justice is pleasing to God. Pure means that we have clean thoughts. We cannot have any doubt or any polluted thoughts come into what we are trying to do. In Psalm 51, David asks God to create in him a clean heart. Ultimately, as an athlete or coach, the goal should be to please God. Therefore, all thoughts and actions should line up with God's word. We have to think positive, because it is praiseworthy, commendable, and an excellent way to think.

No better way than the word of God exists to promote positive self-talk. If these positive thoughts are in our hearts, it will show in our actions. Everyone needs to set aside some time for thinking and meditation on God. By meditating on God's word day and night, His truth and pleasing word gets deep down in our soul. We increase our faith and confidence, and our words and actions line up with the word of God.

2

Purpose

#8: Eternal Purpose

*One of the scribes came near and heard them disputing with one
another, and seeing that he answered them well, he asked him,
"Which commandment is the first of all?" Jesus answered, "The first is,
'Hear, O Israel: love the Lord your God with all your heart, and with all
your soul, and with all your mind, and with all your strength.'"*
—Mark 12:28-30

A relationship with God means you can receive many of the blessings that he has set forth for you and your team. We don't develop a relationship with God to receive worldly blessing, but we do it for an eternal crown. In order to love God, you must love His Son Jesus. God tells us in His word that no one comes to the Father without loving and accepting his son Jesus. In John 14:6-7, God's word says that, "Jesus said to him, I am the way, and the truth, and the life. No one comes to the Father except through me. If you know me, you will know my Father also. From now on you do know him and have seen him."

Once we accept Jesus Christ in our lives, we are saved and have eternal life with God. We truly must believe that Christ died for our sins, and rose from the dead on the third day. Repent of your sins, confess them to God, and ask forgiveness from God. Believe that Jesus died and rose again on the third day and this faith will renew your relationship with God if you are already a believer. If you are not a believer, you now have a relationship with God. In order to be a blessing to your team, you must be right with God. A leader must have a will to serve, not manipulate, his team. Once you are truly walking the walk with Jesus, you will be able to love your team. God will bless you with not only scoreboard wins, but you will be able to win others to eternal victory through your daily servant attitude with your team. You must love God every hour of the day with all of your heart, all of your soul, all of your mind, and all of your strength, including during some of the toughest times, which include practice and tough games/situations.

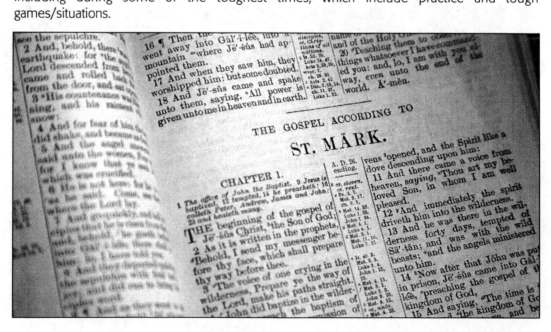

#9: A Brother's Purpose

The second is this, 'You shall love your neighbor as yourself.'
—Mark 12:31

This decree is God's second greatest commandment for us in the Bible, and many times, leaders forget this thought on the way to work or school in the morning. Many live spiritual lives outside their sports and jobs, but fail to control their tongue when dealing with their team. As John Maxwell mentioned in many of his books, "People don't care how much you know until they know how much you care." Many coaches and athletes have what it takes to be successful, but lose their jobs or their positions because they are unable to connect with people or they allow their egos to get in the way. The minute your team senses that you care and love them, they will fight to the end for you. Jesus loved us so much that he laid His life down for us. As servants of God, we must do the same for people we are leading. We are not there to see what our team can do for us, but what we can we do for the team.

The following suggestions can help in caring for others:

- You have to care for yourself before you can care for others.
- Tell your team often that you care for them.
- Spend time getting to know everyone on your team. Find out about their families, major concerns, where they are from, and what's going on in their life.
- Promote teambuilding activities that will make the team bond closer, such as ropes courses, going camping, eating together, and going to church together. Prayer and fellowship will fuel hidden energy in your team morale and spirit.

#10: The Lost Sheep May Be on Your Bench

What do you think? If a shepherd has a hundred sheep, and one of them has gone astray, does he not leave the ninety-nine on the mountains and go in search of the one that went astray? And if he finds it, truly I tell you, he rejoices over it more than over the ninety-nine that never went astray. So it is not the will of your Father in heaven that one of these little ones should be lost.
—Matthew 18:12-14

Once we have God in our life, we have to be as Christ-like as possible. If God would chase after one lost sheep then we must do the same. We often focus on the superstars, and we tend to pay less attention to the not-so-gifted. In the eyes of God, they are all sheep, and if someone on the team goes astray, it is our duty to pull them back in. Whatever the problem is, you should not look for ways to rid the person from the team, but should go bring that person back in with the rest. Without a bench no team exists. Even if the person is not a starter or is not a playmaker, God has placed him on your team. You have to take care of the flock. If you love God, then you love all people. You have to carry this attitude into the locker room, and don't forget the God you serve. In John 21:16 Jesus said, "Tend my sheep," which means we have to take care of all God's people until Christ returns.

#11: Pray for and Love Your Enemies

*But I say to you that listen, Love your enemies, do good to those
who hate you, bless those who curse you, pray for those who
abuse you. If anyone strikes you on the cheek, offer the other also;
and from anyone who takes away your coat do not withhold even
your shirt. Give to everyone who begs from you; and if anyone
takes away your goods, do not ask for them again. Do to others as
you would have them do to you.*
—Luke 6:27-31

As coaches and athletes, we see the teams we play as our enemies. Oftentimes, we think that certain coaches and players on our teams are working against us. God tells us to love everyone, no matter what our conscious may be telling us. We must forgive those who have wronged us. In the Bible, King David loved Saul although Saul wanted to take David's life. We must turn the other cheek when other coaches, opponents, the media, our supervisor, or whoever may be trying to belittle our common good. When I traveled with the Athletes in Action basketball team in South Africa, no matter how rough the play, both teams shook hands and prayed at the conclusion of each game. Once at a football game between Liberty University and Norfolk State University, both teams met at the 50-yard game and prayed together. During the game it was very physical, and there didn't appear to be any love between the two teams.

In Matthew 5:44-45, God says, "But I tell you: Love your enemies and pray for those who persecute you, that you may be sons of your Father in heaven." Our enemies will act the way we act. If we show any kindness then they will follow.

Consider the following saying: "We shall pass through this world but once. If there is any kindness that we can show or do, let us do it now. We may never pass this way again." Those statements have some truth, but remember that we will pass through God's gates someday, and we want to know that we loved everyone, even the so-called enemies that may have brought stress into our lives.

One thing for sure is that an enemy exists who comes to take us out, and that enemy is Satan. We have to keep our guard on at all times for Satan. He comes usually disguised, so we must be detectives of Christ and stop Satan from destroying us and those around us. As leaders, we must prevent the enemy from entering any part of the program. We must teach our team how to deal with the enemy.

#12: Leading a Purpose-Driven, Not Money-Driven, Life

*For the love of money is a root of all kinds of evil, and in their
eagerness to be rich some have wandered away from the faith
and pierced themselves with many pains.*
—1 Timothy 6:10

Editor's Note: This lesson is written specifically for coaches, but the overall message applies to both coaches and athletes.

Money gives us more options in this world, and we are able to contribute more to other people. When you signed your faculty or coaching contract, this amount may have been more money than you ever dreamed about making in any one year or over several years. We tend to live up to the salary that we are making. When we were in college, we could live with almost no disposable income. As our salary rises, we tend to give into the things of this world, such as a bigger office, bigger car, bigger house, and impressive clothes and jewelry, and some of us change the circle of people around us.

It is evident that the love of money is the root of all kinds of evil. We have to remember that it's all God, and he blesses and loves us whether we have money or not. One of the first steps to failing as a leader is holding on to our positions just for the salary. You have to take the position to care for God's people, not because you want to make a six- or seven-figure income. How long you keep that income is determined by God, and it is determined by whether you are taking care of His sheep. Your staff and athletes know when you are there just for the money. There has to be another motivation that wants you to lead ballplayers or lead a staff, or teach students or a congregation, and the love for God, not money, will direct your path to success. In Luke 6:38, God tells us, "Give, and it will be given to you. A good measure, pressed down, shaken together, running over, will be put into your lap; for the measure you give will be the measure you get back." God can double the income where you are, and he can take you higher than you can ever imagine. You first must offer a hand of love to your staff and athletes.

#13: The Coach's Purpose

Train children in the right way, and when old, they will not stray.
—Proverbs 22:6

Editor's Note: This lesson is written specifically for coaches, but the overall message applies to both coaches and athletes.

A coach has to look upon his staff as children of God. Whether you are leading Little League or professional athletes, you have to see them as children of God. You must not withhold strict discipline, and you have to prepare them to live beyond the game. So many athletes have left their game and had nothing to turn to when their careers were over. Sharing your faith, beliefs, and life values will prepare your athletes beyond their senior game and day of retirement. We have all gone back to our hometowns, and we catch up with old buddies that we played on the same team with. Some of these buddies still have not found God, and some are still living and pondering over their high school football statistics. As coaches, you will live through many wins and losses, and whatever happened in high school will be fading memories, not something you are still placing your hats on. One thing that sticks in our minds is the last game we ever played in, and whether we won or lost it stays with us the rest of our life.

For a long time, I dreamed for a state championship in high school baseball. We lost 6-4 in our district championships, and I was the one who made the last out at bat. I struggled with that for a long time. God has provided other moments in my life where I have come up short. Making the last out in baseball was the end, but the beginning to learning that life has ups and downs. What happened today is over. We have to forget about it, and get ready for the next day. Another team is riding in, and they are the only ones who are going to beat us when we are down. When we fall short of winning, whether on the field or in relationships, we must remember that God is training us for something way bigger. We have to teach our kids how to take it on the chin, but get up and continue to fight. Jesus did not stay down, so we must pick up our cross daily and fight life's battles.

I am either up or getting up.
—Unknown

In order to win the fight, I must get off of the mat.
—Unknown

#14: Where Is Your Treasure?

*Do not store up for yourselves treasures on earth, where moth and
rust consume and where thieves break in and steal; but store up
for yourselves treasures in heaven, where neither moth nor rust
consumes and where thieves do not break in and steal. For where
your treasure is, there your heart will be also.*
—Matthew 6:19-21

Editor's Note: This lesson is written specifically for coaches, but the overall message applies to both coaches and athletes.

A leader's heart will focus more on whatever his treasure is. Leaders often get caught up in pleasing today's crowd. I need to please the alumni, management, and the crowd. Sometimes, we try to please ourselves before pleasing those God has put in front of us. We must lay down our life for our athletes and our staff. We can't worry about what the local paper is saying, or what the television media is reporting. If we are taking care of our athletes and staff, God will bless whatever we are leading and serving. If we are just in the job for the money, then our heart is in the wrong place. To paraphrase Matthew 6:21, "Where your treasure is, your heart will follow." Most leaders use their current positions as a stepping stone for a promotion for another position. In Matthew 19:21, "Jesus said to him, 'If you wish to be perfect, go, sell your possessions, and give the money to the poor, and you will have treasure in heaven; then come, follow me.'"

As a coach/leader the most precious thing you can give to your staff and athletes is time. God has asked us all to tithe our money in church, and give offerings to the poor. We must keep promises to the team. If you promise a recruit to pay for his tuition and board through salary, then do it. You can get another athlete, but you can't get your trust and honesty back. If you don't stand by that athlete, he will tell other athletes and recruits you failed to deliver, which will damage your credibility. If you are looking ahead in your career, no way exists to focus on the here and now. We must keep the vision in mind, but we must pick up our cross daily and serve the individuals God has put around us. We must be 100 percent committed to whatever God has called us to do. We can't look back at yesterday, and we can't look ahead to tomorrow. We have to make an impact on who we have in front of us right now. Oftentimes, teams fall to teams that they should have easily beaten, because they are looking ahead. As coaches, we can't look down the schedule, or we can't focus on when the promotion will take place. Things that we ponder on will eventually leak out of our character, and once your athletes know that you are not committed, their effectiveness and desire to follow will level off. Whether you are leading a big staff or small staff, you must give them all that you have.

3

Faith

#15: Run With Faith

Therefore, since we are surrounded by so great a cloud of witnesses,
let us also lay aside every weight and the sin that clings so closely, and
let us run with perseverance the race that is set before us, looking to
Jesus the pioneer and perfecter of our faith, who for the sake of the joy
that was set before Him endured the cross, disregarding its shame,
and has taken His seat at the right hand of the throne of God.
—Hebrews 12:1-2

Every step we take is a faith walk, and every breath we take is a blessing from the Lord. Although, at times, we may seem that we are running this race of life by ourselves, we do have a cloud of witnesses. Just as in a marathon run, a lot of runners start out together, but as the race goes along and the miles add up, everyone is spread out over the race course. The start of the race is marked with loud claps, excitement, and a buzz of enthusiasm. At stations along the way, friends are handing out water and supplements to help their loved ones to finish the race. A great cloud of witnesses is watching.

As the race goes on, the crowd thins out, and at times we may not see the next person who is in front of us. A runner must remove all weight that weighs him down during the course, which symbolizes that in order to run with perseverance, we must get the baggage out of our life, which is when the race gets tough. But we have to remember that we have a great cloud of witnesses, and we know that the Lord Jesus has already won this same race for us. He is cheering us on along with others who have gone before us, and He remembers the hills, the bends in the roads, the competitors along the way, and the challenges that we face. As we look at Hebrews 12:1-2, we too must run with perseverance, just as Jesus did. The course has been set before us, and we will have obstacles to go around and hills to overcome. It is easier to keep going if we focus our minds on the finish line, and as the word says, to look to Jesus to give us the strength to finish strong. Jesus was the pioneer, because He finished the course first and He ran a perfect race. The odds were stacked against him, but He proved to the world that He was God's Son and champion by rising from the dead.

A marathon run can be marked with many challenges. Many people finish the long race, but some individuals give up along the way, and some cramp up on this long journey. Some have perished, and some became injured. We have to set our eyes on Jesus when running the race of life. He endured the cross for us, and he paved a way for us to run this long course. Through God's word and keeping our thoughts on Jesus, we draw closer to the finish line daily. Although we are covered in mud, sweat, tears, and just worn down, we have to remember that Jesus too endured similar shame on the cross. He defeated the shame of common men, and because of His perseverance and unconditional love for us, He is able to pass us the baton.

We must continue the race that Jesus started, and we must get others started. We have a great cloud of witnesses cheering us on, and our number one coach and fan is the Lord and His Son. He has given us the comforter, the Holy Spirit, which is the additional supplement we need to finish the race.

#16: With Faith, We Have Won Before We Have Started

Now faith is the assurance of things hoped for,
the conviction of things not seen.
—Hebrews 11:1

The word faith can be translated into confidence. Confidence is believing in self, a person, or a thing. We believe in God, although we have not seen Him. Confidence comes from our experiences. As we draw closer to God, we gain more confidence in the Lord Jesus Christ. Our faith continues to strengthen, and God tells us that faith comes from hearing the word.

Marcus Garvey once said, "With confidence, we have won even before we have started." We increase our faith by reading and hearing the word of God. Romans 10:17 states, "So faith comes from what is heard, and what is heard comes through the word of Christ." Fellowship and encouragement from others definitely increases our faith. Additionally, when we hear the word of God, our faith magnifies more than what any human can bring to the table. Through conviction, we are able to experience God's will for our life.

Increasing our confidence starts with baby steps. Moses was not confident in his ability to speak to the people, thus he kept asking God to let Aaron speak. God continued to encourage him, and Moses eventually mastered public speaking to the Israelites. Moses was already successful in speaking, because he had been talking with King Pharaoh long before he started instructing the Israelites. It took crafty speech to interface with King Pharaoh, and Moses said the right things every time through God's guidance.

No matter what today brings, we have faith tomorrow. We know that Christ Jesus has won all the battles, and He has gone ahead of us and prepared a place for us. We still have to fight, because the devil also knows that when we accept Christ, we are victorious. The devil comes to kill, steal, and destroy. In John 16:33 Jesus says, "I have said this to you, so that in me you may have peace. In the world you face persecution. But take courage; I have conquered the world." Jesus lets us know that we are going to have trouble, but He has already conquered the world. The devil will deceive, tempt, and bring harm to turn people away from the truth, but Jesus has given us the confidence to win. No matter what we are facing today, the great thing is that we already have a victory. No matter what the scoreboard is reporting, by the time the game is over, we will be in the lead and victorious. Therefore, as we look at the scoreboard of life we may feel that we are losing. Winning is not determined by how many degrees we have, how much we have saved for retirement, and/or how successful our career has been; winning takes place the moment we make Jesus our Lord, and we bring more people on our team.

I know that we have not physically seen Jesus, but we experience Him every time we read the word and fellowship with others. We must hold onto our confidence today, and have a victory shout. We must continue to be confident in our abilities and our success through Christ Jesus, and realize that we must continue to walk by faith and not by sight, and be careful that we are not disqualified after calling others to the field. 1 Corinthians 9:27 states, "But I punish my body and enslave it, so that after proclaiming to others, I myself should not be disqualified."

#17: Lift Your Confidence By Lifting Your Hands

*So Joshua fought the Amalekites as Moses had ordered, and
Moses, Aaron and Hur went to the top of the hill. As long as
Moses held up his hands, the Israelites were winning, but
whenever he lowered his hands, the Amalekites were winning.
When Moses' hands grew tired, they took a stone and put it under
him and he sat on it. Aaron and Hur held his hands up—one on
one side, one on the other—so that his hands remained steady till
sunset. So Joshua overcame the Amalekite army with the sword.*
—Exodus 17:10-13

A boxing coach always encourages athletes to keep their hands up for protection. By having his hands up, the boxer is able to block blows from the opponent. Likewise, a basketball coach encourages his players to keep their hands up while playing defense. Having our hands elevated creates a challenge for the enemy. If a fighter makes it to the later rounds of the fight, his arms will be tired, making it hard to keep his hands up to protect his face. Towards the second half or the fourth quarter of a basketball game, the players' arms will be tired. If we have really practiced for the later rounds and later part of the game, then we will have the stamina to keep our hands up. A greater strength is needed sometimes than our physical strength, and that comes from God alone.

As long as Moses kept his hands up, the Amalekites were winning the battle. As the battle went on, Moses' hands grew tired. Moses had the rod of God in his hands, and sometimes the tasks that God gives us can cause fatigue and heaviness. In order to win, Moses needed to keep his hands elevated. A stone was also propped underneath Moses to keep him up. Similar to Moses, our team can get tired in the battle as well. We sometimes need the fellowship of others. Moses had one person on one side, and another person on the other side to help keep his hands raised. It is important that we have fellowship with others, which helps keep our hands in the air. One thing that gives us the victory daily is raising our hands to God, and giving Him praise and worship. As long as our hands are lifted towards God giving him praise, we can conquer Satan daily and claim the victory that has been laid up for us.

The stone that was placed under Moses was to give him a steady foundation. Our stone is Jesus Christ. He is the cornerstone of all churches, and through Him we have eternal victory and salvation. When our arms are stretched upward toward the heavens like Moses, God sees our faith, and He rains blessings down. When we put our confidence in Jesus, we are victorious, no matter how tough the battle of life.

We must raise our arms to give thanks to the Lord and trust God to help us in the areas of our lives where victory is needed. By lifting our arms, we are surrendering to God, and we are able to look up and take the focus off of what is down. God is up on what we are down on. We should ask ourselves if Jesus is the one thing that is giving us stability in our lives or if we are putting our trust in earthly possessions and shields. We must claim victory by lifting our arms and giving God praise. Rejoice, as we have Jesus, our steady foundation, and He is able to forgive us of our sins and give us the eternal victory.

#18: Faith Should Cause Movement

*In the same way, faith by itself, if it is not accompanied by action,
is dead. But someone will say, "You have faith; I have deeds."
Show me your faith without deeds, and I will show you my faith by
what I do. You believe that there is one God. Good! Even the
demons believe that—and shudder.*
—James 2:17-19

Philippians 4:13 says, "I can do all things through Christ who strengthens me." Putting the words strength and Christ together in a sentence is uplifting and powerful alone. An athlete can say that he is going to do better in the next quarter, next game, and next year. Unless that athlete follows his words with action, his performance will remain the same. It takes work to increase our ability to play whatever sport we are trying to play. Our faith is the same way. Faith requires action, and action requires work and discipline. In order to increase faith, we must continue to read the word of God. Romans 10:17 states that faith also comes through hearing the word of God. We can increase our faith through the encouragement of others.

James 2:17 states that faith without action is dead. Many people will say that they know Christ, but no action exists. The Bible tells us that we will know these individuals by their fruit. A person who is a believer should have good fruit. Galatians 5:22-23 says, "But the fruit of the Spirit is love, joy, peace, patience, kindness, goodness, faithfulness, gentleness, and self-control." Our actions should be revealing good fruit. Old things should be put away, and a new spirit and attitude should be present.

In 2 Corinthians 5:17, God's word says, "Therefore, if anyone is in Christ, he is a new creation; the old has gone, the new has come!" A new creation means that we are doing things that we never did before. It means that the old life should not be present, and we should have a new attitude toward life and others. The person should want to share the good news of Christ with others.

We should do good works for the Lord. In James 2:19, God tells us that even demons believe. Along with our faith, the desire to do God's work should be increased. We do not have to get into ministry full-time, however. Colossians 3:23 says, "Whatever you do, work at it with all your heart, as working for the Lord, not for men, since you know that you will receive an inheritance from the Lord as a reward." We also know that we are saved by grace. Nothing exists that we can do to inherit the kingdom, because we are saved by grace. In Ephesians 2:8-9, God tells us, "For it is by grace you have been saved, through faith—and this not from yourselves, it is the gift of God—not by works, so that no one can boast." An increase in faith will bring an automatic desire to please God. It will not seem like work. We have learned that action is good, but it shouldn't be done as a way to gain favor with God. Our belief in God alone will cause movement to advance the kingdom.

We are saved by grace, meaning that our sins are forgiven and we believe that Jesus died and that He was raised from the dead on the third day. Part of our work is confessing our sins and repenting, and believing that Jesus did rise on the third day. The work is sharing the good news with every person that God has put in our path—not for self glory, but for God's glory.

#19: Unfinished Business

Being confident of this, that he who began a good work in you will
carry it on to completion until the day of Christ Jesus.
—Philippians 1:6

The term WIP stands for "work in progress." If you look at a car in the assembly line, it is a work in progress. When we are baking dinner, it is work in progress. The product is not fully finished, but it is moving toward completion. An artist looks at a block of marble, and sees work in progress. Others may look at it as a large pebble. Think of the great Michelangelo, who took a large boulder that others put on the junk pile and sculptured King David out of it.

God has us in the right place at the right time. Where we are is where we are supposed to be right now. He is the potter, and we are the clay. One thing we must do is keep our eyes fixed on God, and always keep our minds on the finish line. Although the finish line may not be in sight, we have to continue to trust God, and work toward the goals He has set for us. His goals are in the Bible, and obedience to reading, praying, and applying what we learn is essential for moving us forward. Even when we are not being used by God in our eyes, we must know that we are a work in progress. In Philippians 1:6, God says, "Being confident of this, that he who began a good work in you will carry it on to completion until the day of Christ Jesus." God is telling us to stay confident, and be assured that He is going to complete what He started in us. We must live by faith, and not by sight. It is easy to give up in the middle of the race, because we are tired and we perceive so many runners ahead of us. I read a poster once in childhood that stated, "The race is not always to the swift, but keep on running." Peaks and valleys will exist on our journey, but God is telling us to be confident that He is with us the whole way.

In the Bible, we can be inspired by Job. In a short period of time, Job lost his family and all of his earthly possessions. Many of his friends had written him off, but Job never cursed God. He went through periods of depression, and called upon the Lord for a long time with no response from God.

> *The Lord blessed the latter days of Job more than his beginning;*
> *and he had fourteen thousand sheep, six thousand camels, a*
> *thousand yoke of oxen, and a thousand donkeys. He also had seven*
> *sons and three daughters. He named the first Jemimah, the second*
> *Keziah, and the third Keren-happuch. In all the land, there were no*
> *women so beautiful as Job's daughters; and their father gave them*
> *an inheritance along with their brothers. After this, Job lived one*
> *hundred and forty years, and saw his children, and his children's*
> *children, four generations. And Job died, old and full of days.*
> —Job 42:12-17

During most of the book of Job, Job is in distress, and he is a work in progress. But God restored all his earthy possessions, and he still had a full life after his fall. Like Job, our best years are ahead of us, not behind us. God is molding us in his image as we spin on the potter's wheel.

#20: The Faith Walk

And early in the morning he came walking toward them on the sea. But when the disciples saw him walking on the sea, they were terrified, saying, "It is a ghost!" And they cried out in fear. But immediately, Jesus spoke to them and said, "Take heart, it is I; do not be afraid." Peter answered him, "Lord, if it is you, command me to come to you on the water." He said, "Come." So Peter got out of the boat, started walking on the water, and came toward Jesus. But when he noticed the strong wind, he became frightened, and, beginning to sink, he cried out, "Lord save me!" Jesus immediately reached out His hand and caught him, saying to him, "You of little faith, why did you doubt?" When they got into the boat, the wind ceased. And those in the boat worshipped him, saying, "Truly you are the Son of God."
—Matthew 14:25-33

Plenty of athletes choke when the big game or tournament is on the line. Sometimes, the entire team chokes or becomes fearful. It is hard to be victorious at anything when we have even a grain of fear in our body. In Proverbs 1:7, God tells us, "The fear of the Lord is the beginning of knowledge; fools despise wisdom and instruction."

The only one we should fear is God. No circumstance or no one should cause us to stumble. Sometimes, just a moment of hesitation can cause failure. Oftentimes, basketball players miss the game-winning shot because of nervousness, and in the business world, leaders sometimes struggle with success. Peter was walking on water, and he was in a zone. But he was distracted by the wind. Oftentimes, something will come along and pull us away from our strength zone. Perhaps, if Peter had stayed focused, he could have made it all the way to Jesus on the water. Matthew 14:32 states that the wind ceased once Peter got in the boat. The wind was a teaser, and maybe just the one thing to cause him to stumble. When we are walking in faith, we must stay focused. Other deterrents will be present, similar to the wind, such as material things, ungodly relationships, greed, fame, and pride. Peter could have done the possible, but because he lost focus and paid attention to the wind, the faith walk seemed impossible.

The one thing that we can learn from Peter is that we can do the impossible by staying focused. He did walk for a little while on top of the water, which is the impossible. When God calls us out on the water, we must not doubt what He is calling us to do. We must walk by faith, and not by sight. God has given us many impossible things to do. He woke us up this morning. He allowed us to bathe and serve ourselves breakfast. He permitted our car to start, and He gave us breath and a heartbeat. The impossible things are the breath and the heartbeat, which are life.

As we move forward in the journey of life, we should not be distracted by the wind. We need to stay focused, and not be distracted by fear. We know that faith as small as a mustard seed can move mountains. If something is distracting you, say this prayer: "Lord, I give you praise now and I thank you for the faith and I will only fear you. I thank you for Jesus today, amen."

#21: The Confidence Factor

Then Samson called to the Lord and said, "Lord God, remember me and strengthen me only this once, O God, so that with this one act of revenge I may pay back the Philistines for my two eyes. And Sampson grasped the two middle pillars on which the house rested, and he leaned his weight against them, his right hand on the one, and his left hand on the other. Then Samson said, "Let me die with the Philistines." He strained with all his might and the house fell on the lords and all the people who were in it. So those he killed at his death were more than those he had killed during his life.
—Judges 16:28-30

Sampson was known for his great strength. An angel had told Samson's mother that he was to never cut his hair. It was a symbolic form of strength for Samson. He was promised to deliver Israel from the hands of the Philistines. They had been in captivity for 40 years. At times, Samson actually may have been overconfident. He did not listen to his parents, and he married a woman from another tribe. He wanted what pleased himself, even if it didn't always line up with God. After Samson killed 1,000 Philistines with the jawbone of a donkey, he demanded the Lord to give him water after the victory.

By then he was very thirsty, and he called on the Lord, saying, "You have granted this great victory by the hand of your servant. Am I now to die of thirst, and fall into the hands of the uncircumcised?" So God split open the hollow place that is at Lehi, and water came from it. When he drank, his spirit returned, and he revived.
—Judges 15:18-19

But Samson eventually met his match. Delilah begged Samson, asking where his strength came from. He finally told her that it was his hair, and if his hair would ever be cut, then he would be powerless. The Philistines seized him, and shaved his head. They poked out his eyes, and made fun of him. In Judges 16:28, Samson asked God one time to restore his strength. What the Philistines failed to realize was that Samson's hair had grown back and his confidence was restored. He was able to bring the pillars down and defeat the Philistines at the end.

Was it Samson's hair that gave him strength or was it the prayer? Many people put their strength and power in their physical being or material possessions, but the true confidence factor resides in prayer. When Sampson prayed, and asked God to give him his strength, the Lord answered his prayers, allowing him to defeat the Philistines. The Bible says, "He strained with all his might." Like Samson, once we pray and ask God for strength, we must strain forward. Philippians 3:13 states, "Beloved, I do not consider that I have made it my own; but this one thing I do: forgetting what lies behind and straining forward to what lies ahead, I press on toward the goal for the prize of the heavenly call of God in Christ Jesus." We must not look back, and we must strain forward for what God has for us. Think about what you are looking back at today that may have defeated you and what you need to pray about and give to God so you can move forward. The confidence factor starts with prayer, and then putting our strength to action.

4

Fear

#22: Worry and Anxiety

Do not be anxious about anything, but in everything, by prayer
and petition, with thanksgiving, present your requests to God.
—Philippians 4:6

God tells us to rejoice in Him always. As long as we can stay focused on God, we will not get caught up in the cares of this world.

The story of Peter comes to mind when discussing worry and stress. Jesus was on the lake, and He asked Peter to walk on the water toward Him. Peter got out of the boat, and started walking toward Jesus, and when the wind distracted him, he immediately began to sink. Individuals react to distractions the same way. As soon as trouble comes, we forget the power that we have inside of us. Peter began to sink, but Jesus was there to save him. Like Peter, we forget who has called us to step out on faith. Jesus will pull us up too when we fall. We can walk further than Peter on water as long as we trust God in our circumstances. Worry eventually leads us to sin, because we do not have faith in God. In Matthew 6:34, God's word says, "Don't worry about tomorrow, for tomorrow will bring its own worries. Today's trouble is enough for today." The blowing of the wind distracted Peter. Some of our distractions (like the wind in Peter's case) are people, finances, an abusive spouse, friendships, job, school, and life clutter. As long as we keep our eyes fixed on Jesus, we will stay afloat in life.

We should never stress over basic necessities. In Matthew 6:24, God promises us that we will have food, clothing, and a place to stay. In Matthew 6:25-27, God says, "Therefore I tell you, do not worry about your life, what you will eat or drink; or about your body, what you will wear. Is not life more important than food, and the body more important than clothes? Look at the birds of the air; they do not sow or reap or store away in barns, and yet your heavenly Father feeds them. Are you not much more valuable than they? Who of you by worrying can add a single hour to his life?" God is telling us that we are much more important than the birds of the air, and He provides for the birds. In Matthew 6:28-29, He even talks about how He allows the flowers to bloom. God's word says, "And why do you worry about clothes? See how the lilies of the field grow. They do not labor or spin. Yet I tell you that not even Solomon in all his splendor was dressed like one of these."

The enemy will cause worry by attacking our health. We just have to remember the many miracles Jesus performed on the sick. A woman just touched the hem of Jesus' garment, and her bleeding problem of 12 years ceased (Mark 5:25-34). In another situation, some men who couldn't get to Jesus, due to the full church, climbed on the roof, and cut a hole through which they let a paralyzed man down to be near Jesus (Luke 5:17-26). Jesus healed him because of the faith of the man. All we need to do is stay near Jesus to keep our confidence. His word says that if we have faith as small as a mustard seed, we can speak to a mountain and move it into the sea. It is through faith, and not of ourselves, that we have been saved. In Hebrews 11:1, God says, "Now faith is being sure of what we hope for and certain of what we do not see. This is what the ancients were commended for." We have to be confident that Jesus did die for us, and through believing in His resurrection we have eternal life with God. Jesus has already overcome the world for us, so we do not have to worry about this life. In James 1:6, God says, "But when he asks, he must believe and not doubt, because he who doubts is like a wave of the sea, blown and tossed by the wind." We can't be lukewarm in our prayers or our faith. In Revelation 3:16-17, Jesus said to us, "So, because you are lukewarm—neither hot nor cold—I am about to spit you out of my mouth. You say I am rich; I have acquired wealth and do not need a thing. But you do not realize that you are wretched, pitiful, poor, blind and naked." We have to keep our trust in God. We need to focus on today, and let tomorrow worry about itself.

#23: Keep Your Eyes on the Hills

I lift up my eyes to the hills—where does my help come from? My help comes from the Lord, the maker of heaven and earth. He will not let your foot slip—he who watches over you will not slumber; indeed, he who watches over Israel will neither slumber nor sleep. The Lord watches over you—the Lord is your shade at your right hand; the sun will not harm you by day or the moon by night. The Lord will keep you from all harm—He will watch over your life; the Lord will watch over your coming and going both now and forevermore.
—Psalm 121:1-8

As we can see from this passage, we have nothing to worry about. God says just lift our eyes up toward the hills, and our help will come from Him. God says that he will be our shade by day, and protect us at night. He will protect us from evil. Remember the three wise men that showed up at the birth of Jesus. As they were leaving, the angels of God came and warned them not to return back to the King Pharaoh. King Pharaoh was jealous of the birth of Jesus Christ, and it was believed that he would probably harm the men who came to worship Jesus. However, because the wise men were honoring God's Son, He protected them. We have so much to thank God for every day. Sometimes, we take a different route home, and later we hear that a tragic accident occurred on the path that we were on. God orders our steps, and He will protect us forevermore. He will not allow us to be harmed. He has a purpose for our life— we should give Him praise.

#24: Calm My Storm

One day, Jesus said to his disciples, "Let's go over to the other side of the lake." So they got into a boat and set out. As they sailed, he fell asleep. A squall came down on the lake, so that the boat was being swamped, and they were in great danger. The disciples went and woke him, saying, "Master, master, we're going to drown!" He got up and rebuked the wind and the raging waters; the storm subsided, and all was calm. "Where is your faith?" He asked his disciples. In fear and amazement they asked one another, "Who is this? He commands even the winds and the water, and they obey him."
—Luke 8:22-25

We have a choice as to whether we rely on God's strength or our own strength. It's important that we stay close to God in prayer and fellowship. Oftentimes, we are going along without giving Him the glory for our daily walk of life. We wait until a moment of crisis before we look for God. Although we think that God's hands are not on us when problems come, He says that He will not fall asleep on us.

The disciples were all stressing out during the storm, and they perceived Jesus to be asleep. He is the Son of God—He knows what is going on. He was testing their faith. We are much like the disciples when storms or trials hit our life. We hit the panic button, and we start calling on Jesus. Perhaps if the disciples had talked to Jesus along the way, He may have not fallen asleep on the boat. We ignore Jesus just like the disciples did. We are busy with the cares of this world, and we do not give God enough praise. But He is a passionate God, and He loves us unconditionally.

Once, I was on a plane ride when, all of a sudden, the pilot came on the microphone and said that we were going to hit some turbulence. The turbulence came suddenly, tossing the plane around. I became afraid, more than I could handle. I watched the faces of the other people on the plane, and they were looking frightened as well. I looked up at the airline attendant, and she could tell that I was nervous. She took it in stride. She kept smiling, and she sent a signal that everything was going to be okay. I wondered if she was feeling the turbulence and if she was frightened. This attendant had probably been through many storms or turbulence more severe than this incident. I didn't realize how scared I really was, and then I started to pray and I said to God, "If this is it, then your will be done." I started thinking of all the things that I have not accomplished in life, and finally the pilot spoke on the microphone, "We are five minutes from our destination, and we will continue to experience some bumps along the way." But I received a feeling of assurance. Before I knew it, we were touching down on the ground.

The plane ride was so bumpy, and my stomach was disturbed by the jolting of the plane and my nervous reaction. The storm was over now, and things were calm. It was something about the prayer that gave me a comfort that everything was going to be all right. It was something about the smile and confidence of the airline attendant that got me through that bumpy moment. Like the disciples in the boat, Jesus will calm our storm. When storms come, He is there for us. He breaks His rest to help us. Perhaps Jesus brought the storm so the disciples would humble themselves. I don't know why I experienced the turbulence in the airplane, but I got a new perspective and I drew closer to God. I actually thanked God for the plane ride. I had a new feeling toward God, and I realized how vulnerable life is.

When I was several thousand feet in the air, and getting tossed around, the only thing I could depend on was the pilot, and I prayed that he had experience with the storm that he was facing. Oftentimes, we put our trust in others to direct our lives, and they let us down. But when we put our trust in God, He calms our storm no matter the situation.

#25: His Hand Will Be There

So He said, "Come." And when Peter had come down out of the boat, he walked on the water to go to Jesus. But when he saw that the wind was boisterous, he was afraid; and beginning to sink he cried out saying, "Lord, save me!" Immediately, Jesus stretched out His hand and caught him, and said to him, "O you of little faith, why did you doubt?" And when they got into the boat, the wind ceased. Then those who were in the boat came and worshiped Him, saying, "Truly you are the Son of God."
—Matthew 14:29-33

The disciples were out on the water when Jesus started coming toward them. He was walking on the water, which frightened the disciples. They perceived him as a ghost. Jesus got closer to the disciples and He comforted them. He told them not to be afraid, and He asked Peter to walk toward Him on the water. Peter got out of the boat and started walking toward Jesus. Peter was amazed because he was accomplishing something that he had no faith in doing. His eyes were fixed on Jesus, and he was so happy because he was doing the impossible. The other disciples were cheering him on, because they also were impressed that Jesus was walking on water. Suddenly, Peter "saw that the wind was boisterous" and he began to sink. He lost his confidence in the midst of his accomplishment. Just for a moment, Peter took His eyes off of Jesus to see the storm, and He lost his footing in the water. Then Jesus reached down, and offered Peter a hand in his fall.

We are much like Peter. We go through life accomplishing tasks, and other believers are impressed at our commitment to God. We too take our eyes off Jesus at times, because of distractions. Oftentimes, we are distracted by the cares of this world, and we can get caught up in the diversions. Some of the distractions that cause us to lose heart and sink like Peter are: we may have an incident on our job, we may not get a decision to go our way at church, or we may get a big bill in the mail, and we worry about how we are going to pay it. The great news is that Jesus always extends a hand to us, and He picks us up out of our sin and our daily falls. When we are sinking, He offers a helping hand to bring us back. Jesus is our life jacket in any circumstance.

We have to take his hand when He extends it to us. Jesus can calm our storms, and He can prevent us from drowning. He is our lighthouse in the storm. He tells us in 1 Peter 5:7 to cast all our cares upon Him. We need to trust Jesus in the storms of life—Jesus is in our boat. If we are sinking in sin or caught up in the cares of this world, His hand is there for us. We need to catch hold of His hand and receive His eternal blessing.

#26: Run Back to Victory

Go back the way you came, and travel to the wilderness of Damascus.
When you arrive there, anoint Hazel to be king of Aram.
—1 Kings 19:15

Even after victory, we can develop fear and worry in our life. Even the prophet Elijah felt fear after his great victory against King Ahab. God had spoken to Elijah, and asked him to report to King Ahab that there would be a drought in the land because the people were following a false God. 1 Kings 17:1 says, "Now Elijah, who was from Tishbe in Gilead, told King Ahab, 'As surely as the Lord, the God of Israel, lives—the God whom I worship and serve—there will be no dew or rain during the next few years unless I give the word!'" After that, God instructed Elijah to hide in the Kerith Brook, because the King would have tried to kill him because of the report He gave. God was protecting him, because He was obeying God.

The drought went on for three years. Crops died, nothing could grow, and the fields were barren. All the streams were dried up. Then God spoke to Elijah in 1 Kings 18:1 saying, "Go and present yourself to King Ahab. Tell him that I will soon send rain." So Elijah went to appear before Ahab and sent message by a servant of the Lord Obadiah to let King Ahab know that he wanted to meet. Obadiah was a man of God, as he had previously hid 100 prophets from the evil Jezebel, who tried to kill all of God's prophets. Obadiah was afraid to report to King Ahab, because he was fearful that Elijah would run after he took the message, putting Obadiah's life in danger for lying to the king. A heavy bounty was on Elijah's head, because he had brought the news about the drought. Elijah promised that he would meet the king, and Obadiah obeyed the prophet Elijah.

Elijah met with the King, and the King referred to him as a troublemaker for causing the drought. And the Prophet Elijah responded in 1 Kings 18:18-19, "I have made no trouble for Israel. You and your family are the troublemakers, for you have refused to obey the commands of the Lord and have worshipped the images of Baal instead. Now bring all the People of Israel to Mount Carmel, with all 450 prophets of Baal and the 400 prophets of Asherah, who are supported by Jezebel."

In 1 Kings 18:21, Elijah said to the people, "How long are you going to waver between two opinions? If the Lord is God, follow him. But if Baal is God, then follow him." But the people were completely silent.

Then Elijah asked for two bulls to be presented, and he allowed them to choose whichever bull they wanted. They cut the bull to pieces and laid them on two separate altars. Elijah challenged them to call on their god Baal to set their bull on fire, and Elijah called on the God of all things. Elijah stated that whoever God answered by setting fire to the wood and sacrifice was the true God. And the people agreed.

Elijah allowed for the prophets of Baal to go first. They placed their bull on their altar, and called out to their god Baal. They received no reply, and Elijah started taunting them. 1 Kings 18:27 states, "About noontime Elijah began mocking them. 'You'll have to shout louder,' he scoffed, 'for surely he is a god! Perhaps he is deep in thought, or he is relieving himself. Or maybe he is away on a trip, or he is asleep and needs to be wakened!'"

Some of the prophets even cut themselves with knives and blood to get their god's attention. Finally, God called to the people, and told them to come to Him. They watched Elijah as he prepared his altar. He used 12 stones to represent the 12 stones of Israel. He used the stones to rebuild the altar of the Lord that had been torn down. Elijah also had them pour water on the bull sacrifice so they would not think that it was fixed or his sacrifice was tampered with. In 1 Kings 18:36-37, at the customary time for offering the evening sacrifice, Elijah said this prayer to the Lord: "O Lord, God of Abraham, Isaac and Jacob, prove today that you are God in Israel and that I am your servant. Prove that I have done all this at your command. O Lord, answer me! Answer me so these people will know that you, O Lord are God and that you have brought them back to yourself."

Immediately, the fire of the Lord flashed down from heaven and burned up the young bull, the wood, the stones, and the dust. It even licked up all the water in the ditch. And when the people saw it, they fell on their faces and cried out, "The Lord is God! The Lord is God!"

The people seized all the prophets of Baal, and killed them. One man of God defeated 450 false prophets that day and brought glory to God. With God on your side, you are never the underdog in your own mind. You can conquer any challenge or opposition. Shortly after that incident, Elijah climbed to the top of Mount Carmel and prayed, and he told his servant to go look out to the sea. The servant saw nothing. Elijah sent him back seven times to look again. On the seventh time, the servant saw a small cloud. Remember, it had not rained in three years. 1 Kings 18:41 says that Elijah instructed the King to prepare a great feast, because rain was coming. Since Elijah had won the battle, the King was listening to him. It rained that day.

Ahab went home and told Jezebel about what Elijah had done. In 1 Kings 19:2, Jezebel sent a message to Elijah to say, "May the gods also kill me if by this time tomorrow I have failed to take your life like those whom you killed." Elijah was afraid and fled for his life. He went to Beersheba, a town in Judah, and he left his servant there. Then he went on alone into the desert, traveling all day. He sat down under a solitary broom tree and prayed that he might die. In 1 Kings 19:4 he says, "I have had enough, Lord. Take my life, for I am no better than my ancestors." How could Elijah, who had just won a major victory, now fall into depression and give up?

This sort of scenario happens all the time. Many times after we are victorious, we forget what God has done for us in the past. You would think that after defeating 450 prophets and bringing rain to the people that Elijah would not fear anything. We may wonder how Tyson loses to Buster Douglas or how USC gets defeated by an underdog—it's fear. We sometimes take our enemy too lightly, or we take our eyes off God just for a moment, which allows the enemy to tear down our faith.

Elijah was lying beside a tree in the desert, and he wanted to die. But God never leaves us when we are in this state of mind. The battle is not ours. An angel of the Lord woke up Elijah and fed him and provided drink. Elijah then got up and traveled for 40 days and 40 nights to Mount Sinai, the mountain of God. He spent the night in a cave there. God spoke to him, "What are you doing here, Elijah?" God commanded Elijah to stand out on the mountain, and caused a mighty windstorm to take place. God asked him again in 1 Kings 19:13, "What are you doing here, Elijah?" Elijah mentioned again that he feared for his life. In 1 Kings 19:15 God tells him,

"Go back the way you came, and travel to the wilderness of Damascus. When you arrive there, anoint Hazel to be king of Aram."

We have all been in Elijah's shoes. We have faced adversity shortly after a great victory. Many teams win the Super Bowl or the World Series, but they find it hard to repeat as champions. We may wonder why God allowed fear to overcome Elijah after the great victory at Mount Carmel. Perhaps, Elijah needed to be humbled, or maybe God was testing him. One thing for sure is we must remember what God has done for us in the past when we were faced with adversity. He allowed us to live through yesterday, and that is a victory today. He gave us His son Jesus, and no matter what we are facing today, that gift brings victory.

God is telling us to go back the way we came. If we have given up on a dream, then we need to go back to it. God will allow others to be blessed by our testimonies and our victories. God commands Elijah to go anoint new kings and a new prophet Elisha. Thus, he goes from depression to crowning kings and anointing new prophets. God will make us victorious again. We have to keep trusting him, even in our depression or down time. The servant had to go to the sea seven times before he saw the cloud. We need to hang on for what we are trusting God for. He will rain for us as well—just keep trusting in him and doing his work. He will have us crowning kings and anointing other disciples.

#27: Thy Will Be Done

He went on a little farther and fell face down on the ground,
praying, "My Father! If it is possible, let this cup of suffering be
taken away from me. Yet I want your will, not mine."
—Matthew 26:39

In this situation, we see that Jesus is faced with the spirit of worry. But we know that Jesus was a perfect sacrifice, and he never sinned. Right away, He says to God, "I want your will to be done, and not my will to be done," which is how we should face worry. When we feel the spirit of worry (anxiety), we must respond like Jesus did. Jesus knew that He had to die at some point, and He knew that it was God's will. He did ask God if it was His will to remove the cup of suffering. The great thing is that He said your will. When we are faced with a trial of suffering, we should say, "God, your will be done."

We often fail forward. When we face a trial, our true character is revealed. We should not grumble as the Israelites in the desert when they were short of manna or bread. Oftentimes, we handle adversity by sprinting across the desert like Elijah running for our life. We don't want to face the thing that may help us in the long run.

Jesus had faith, and He knew that God would raise Him on the third day after His death. That's why we have to follow Jesus Christ, because He bore the cross for us and He died for us. When the cup faces us, we want to try to hold on to this life. God tells us in the word that if you want to save your life you have to lose your life. Jesus remembered this command. We know that a reward is waiting up ahead for us, no matter what trial we are facing.

I had a coach who mentioned that when a loved one passes on we are sad, but we should be rejoicing because that person is now going on to receive his reward if he has lived a life for God. We are like the disciples who didn't want Jesus to die. The disciples wanted Him to stay, but in order to bless us, He had to die to raise himself and others. When we look at this situation in this manner, we can turn tears to smiles and joy. Jesus was in prayer when Judas and the men came for Him. We have to be like Jesus, and stay in prayer. No one knows the day, the time, or the hour, but we need to always be ready.

Ephesians 6:11 says that whatever you are facing, you should "put on the full armor of God," and 1 Timothy 6:12 says, "Fight the good fight." Just know that God will not take us until He has allowed us to start down our road of purpose. Because of our sin nature, we can't live forever and be perfect (Matthew 5:48), but we can maximize our efforts on this earth to be as Christ-like as possible. Therefore, shout when a trial comes because God is getting ready to bless you.

On the other side of a cold or flu, we feel renewed. After coming out of a trial, we always have a better perspective. In James 1:2-3, God says, "Dear brothers and sisters, whenever trouble comes your way, let it be an opportunity for joy. For when your faith is tested, your endurance has a chance to grow." So let it grow, for when your endurance is fully developed, you will be strong in character and ready for anything. We should be joyful when we are faced with opposition. Like Jesus, we can't worry about what we are facing. We just have to say, "Not my will, but God, your will be done." Whatever the outcome, we know that we are victorious before we enter a tight spot. If we keep taking a test, eventually we will pass. That is why we may have to endure the same test or various tests, because God wants to make sure we are ready for the promotion. We need to be ready for our cup when it comes, and although there will be pain and suffering, there will be a place at the right hand of God.

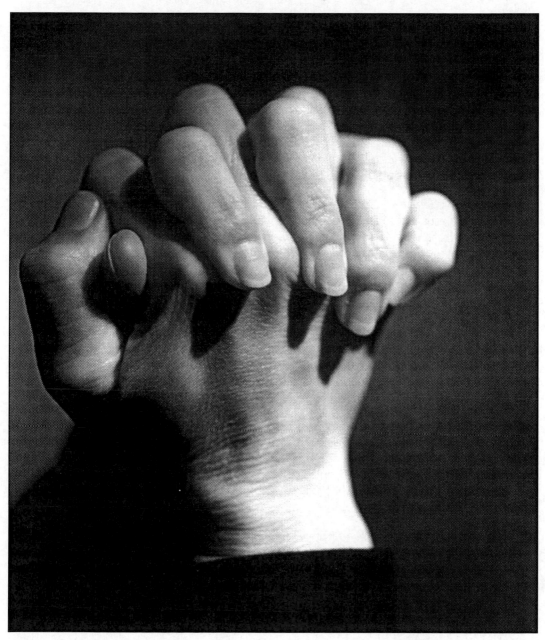

#28: Raven's Food

Then the Lord said to Elijah, "Go to the east and hide by Kerith Brook at a place east of where it enters the Jordan River. Drink from the brook and eat what the ravens bring you, for I have commanded them to bring you food."
—1 Kings 17:2-4

As long as we obey God, He will provide for our basic needs. God knows our dreams, and He directs our paths. He will not let us stumble. As discussed in #26: Run Back to Victory, Elijah prophesied a drought, which would cause a famine. This famine was going to affect Elijah as well. Elijah had to lean on God and trust Him. He had to totally rely on God, and he had to humble himself. He had to live off what the birds brought to him. In the New Testament, God reminds us in Matthew 6:24 that He will even provide for the birds of the air. Sometimes, it's hard to receive from others, because we have been hurt or we are faced with fear. Elijah was being hidden by God, because he was faced with death because of the prophecy. He had told them about the three-year drought, and the land was holding him responsible. God brought the drought because the people believed in the false god Baal.

Many people are afraid to stand up like Elijah. God equips us as Christians to tell others the good news of Jesus Christ, and asks others to repent and turn away from their sins, which is basically what Elijah was doing—he was just working before Christ came. We already know the good news, but yet we hide and are afraid to prophesy for God, due to losing our life, our job, our friends, or our status. Just like Elijah, God will provide manna for us. When Moses was in the desert, God rained down manna for him and the Israelites. He also brought them water.

If we are facing a drought today, we have to trust that God knows our condition, and He will provide for us if we are open to receive it. This situation should not be just a monetary thing. It could be just receiving God's words from others, then taking those words and transforming a portion of our life. It could mean allowing someone of lesser position or job status to help us. Even Elijah had to be meek by relying on his food source from the ravens.

God hid Elijah in this time of danger and drought, and He will do the same when we are facing danger. He will show us a way of escape, and He will provide for us. We just can't get anxious, and run ahead of God. We also witnessed where the same Elijah sprinted across the desert in fear. Philippians 4:6-7 reads, "Don't worry about anything; instead, pray about everything. Tell God what you need, and then thank Him for all He has done. If you do this, you will experience God's peace, which is far more wonderful than the human mind can understand. His peace will guard your hearts and minds as you live in Christ Jesus."

God also told Elijah to drink from the brook of water as well as receive his food from the ravens. Running water symbolizes the Holy Spirit. The word of God is our running water. As long as we are reading and praying on God's word, our needs are going to be met and we will have nothing to fear. We must be obedient to God's command.

God later asked Elijah to go live with a widow and her son. This great prophet had to humble himself again, and ask her for her last serving. The word says in 1 Kings 17:10-12, "So he went to Zarephath. As he arrived at the gates of the village, he saw a widow gathering sticks, and he asked her, 'Would you please bring me a cup of water?' As she was going to get it, he called to her, 'Bring me a bite of bread, too,' But she said, 'I swear by the Lord your God that I don't have a single piece of bread in the house. And I have only a handful of flour left in the jar and a little cooking oil in the bottom of the jug. I was just gathering a few sticks to cook this last meal, and then my son and I will die.'"

Elijah encouraged her to cook that last meal, and he still demanded bread from this woman who wanted to eat her last meal and die. The drought in the land was having a major effect. He comforted her and told her that it would be enough food after she prepared a meal for him first. He also told her that there would always be enough food and oil until the rain came. The woman prepared the meal for him, and just as Elijah had said, the food and oil never ran out.

Later, anxiety fell upon the woman again as her son fell sick. He grew worse, and he finally died. She makes these remarks to Elijah in 1 Kings 17:18: "O man of God, what have you done to me? Have you come to punish my sins by killing my son?" But Elijah replied, "Give me your son." Elijah took the child up to the upper room and stretched him on the bed. He also cried out to the Lord, and he stretched himself out over the child three times and the life of the child came back.

In 1 Kings 17:24 the woman responded, "Now I know for sure that you are a man of God, and that the Lord truly speaks through you." This situation was amazing! The woman doubted God even after Elijah provided a miracle, and allowed for her food not to run out. She did one thing that many fail to do—she gave everything she had to God. Everything at that moment was her last meal and oil for cooking, which she gave to the prophet Elijah. She gave in faith, and God later remember her.

Sometimes, we are hit where it hurts. Her son was sick and he died. Death has a terrible sting, and sometimes we have a blaming spirit. She blamed Elijah for her son's death, because he was there. She was looking for all her needs to be met by the prophet. Elijah performed a great miracle by reviving her son back to life, and the woman's faith was strong again.

This situation is symbolic of Jesus. Mary and the disciples were lowered in spirit when Jesus died. Just like Elijah stretching over the widow's son for three days and reviving him on the third attempt, God raised His son on the third day. He renewed all our faith and saved us all from death by raising Jesus on the third day. Mary and the disciples were brokenhearted as well, until they saw the cornerstone rolled back. Jesus was born to save us, and He died so that we may live.

We should put God first in everything we do, and He will provide for all our needs. We must not be selfish, and we should give God praise. We have so much to be thankful for. He has Jesus in the upper room, and He has prepared a place for us. He is the great star and wonderful counselor. He is all the bread and oil we need and His grace will never run out.

1 Corinthians 2:9, states, "No eye has seen, no ear has heard, and no mind has imagined what God has prepared for those who love him." 1 Corinthians 2:10, goes on to say, "But we know these things because God has revealed them to us by His spirit, and His spirit searches out everything and shows us even God's deep secrets." It is so wonderful to partner with God, because He reveals His secrets to us. We know His deepest secret is that His Son Jesus died for our sins, and through believing in Him, we have eternal life with God. We know that repentance and forgiveness cleanses us, and we are able to share in the grace of the free gift of God's grace.

5

Pride

#29: Purple Pride

There was a certain rich man who was splendidly clothed in purple and fine linen and who lived each day in luxury. At his gate lay a poor man named Lazarus who was covered with sores. As Lazarus lay there longing for scraps from the rich man's table, the dogs would come and lick his open sores. Finally, the poor man died and was carried by the angels to be with Abraham. The rich man also died and was buried, and his soul went to the place of the dead. There, in torment, he saw Abraham in the far distance with Lazarus at his side.
—Luke 16:19-23

In the passage, Jesus states that a "certain" rich man was splendidly clothed. The word "certain" lets us know that not all rich people will be put in eternal torment. Rich does not always mean that we are abundant in money and material things. The rich man may have been in abundance financially, but he was poor in spiritual abundance. The "certain" rich man could have at least shared God's word with the poor man Lazarus. Even if he had just given the word, that would have been enough.

One thing is for sure. No matter how many resources both men had, they both had to die and be judged. The Bible tells us that the rich man died and went to be with the dead, and the poor man was carried up by the angels. Later, the rich man is talking to Abraham from amongst the dead, and he tells Abraham to please tell his brothers to get right with God, because he didn't want them to end up in his state. The Bible also states that the rich man is now poor in resources and the poor man has been blessed in the afterlife.

Luke 16:24-25 goes on to say, "The rich man shouted, 'Father Abraham, have some pity! Send Lazarus over here to dip the tip of his finger in water and cool my tongue. I am in anguish in these flames.' But Abraham said to him, 'Son, remember that during your lifetime you had everything you wanted, and Lazarus had nothing. So now he is here being comforted, and you are in anguish.'"

When people pass by the homeless or less fortunate they don't always give without judging. Some people think that if they give to a less fortunate person, he will probably just buy drugs or alcohol. God tells us that he will come when we least expect it. Surely, the rich man dressed in purple possibly had an attitude that if he gave to the beggar, then he would probably just waste his resources. Perhaps the rich man's pride kept him from even associating with the poor man Lazarus.

Matthew 19:30 states, "But many who are the greatest now will be least important then, and those who seem least important now will be the greatest then." We should think about who we can bless today. Maybe we are in a Lazarus position on this earth. God will send comfort even if it comes from a dog. The Bible states how the dogs would come and lick the sores of the man. More than that, God will send his angels like he did for Lazarus on the final day. We should make a decision to be with the Lord, and continue to bless others who are less fortunate.

#30: Pride Is On the Hit List

There are six things the Lord hates—no, seven things he detests: haughty eyes, a lying tongue, hands that kill the innocent, a heart that plots evil, feet that race to do wrong, a false witness who pours out lies, and a person who sows discord in a family.
—Proverbs 6:16-19

Many leaders in the Bible have fallen from their throne because they let pride get in the way. Pride gets in the way of forgiveness, love, giving, and it can be a hindrance to the fruit of the spirit. In Proverbs 16:19 God gives seven things that He hates and pride is the first one on the list. The definition of haughty means proud, snobbish, scornfully arrogant, and prideful. Satan, our enemy, was cast from the presence of God because of "pride."

Pride also makes up a part of the next six things in the Bible that God says that He hates. Pride is a part of lying and gossip as well because the person who is doing the lying or gossiping may be jealous. When we talk about someone behind his back, we are saying things about that person without his permission. We are not giving that person the opportunity to defend himself.

One of the first forms of pride is seen earlier in the Bible when the innocent is killed. Genesis 4:8-9 states, "One day Cain suggested to his brother, 'Let's go out into the fields.' And while they were in the field, Cain attacked his brother, Abel, and killed him. Afterward, the Lord asked Cain, 'Where is your brother? Where is Abel?' 'I don't know,' Cain responded. 'Am I my brother's guardian?'" Cain killed his own brother, because he was prideful. He was jealous that the Lord had accepted the first fruit of Abel, and that the Lord was not pleased with his offering. Cain had to plot this evil in his heart, and God tells us in Proverbs 6:16-19 that he hates a heart that plots evil. The fifth thing despised by God is feet that race to do wrong. In the same story in Genesis, Cain raced to slay his brother soon after God was more pleased with Abel's offering.

The last thing that God hates is a person who causes discord in his family. A person should provide for his own household, and disagreements in the family can result from pride. A man should submit to his wife, and a wife to her husband. Ephesians 5:22-25 states, "For wives, this means submit to your husbands as to the Lord. For a husband is the head of his wife as Christ is the head of the church. He is the Savior of his body, the church. As the church submits to Christ, so you wives should submit to your husbands in everything. For husbands, this means love your wives, just as Christ loved the church. He gave up his life for her." A person who commits adultery does so in pride. He is not only rebelling against himself, he is rebelling against God.

If we are jealous of anyone, are gossiping or lying to others, or have any confusion in our own home, we should say this prayer: "Lord, thank you for salvation and we ask that you give us a spirit of humility, and help us consider changing if we have even one cell in our body that is prideful in nature."

#31: Washed—Seven Times a Charm

But his officers tried to reason with him and said, "Sir, if the prophet had told you to do something very difficult, wouldn't you have done it? So you should certainly obey him when he says simply, 'Go and wash and be cured!'" So Naaman went down to the Jordan River and dipped himself seven times, as the man of God had instructed him. And his skin became as healthy as the skin of a young child's, and he was healed!
—2 Kings 5:13-14

In the Bible, the number seven often represents completeness. Genesis 2:3 says, "God created the world in six days, and He rested on the seventh day." In Genesis 41, when Joseph interpreted the dreams of King Pharaoh, he said that there would be seven years of plenty, and seven years of famine. In 2 Kings 5:10, Naaman is told that he will be healed on the seventh time in the water. It would take a bit of humility on Naaman's part before he could be healed. He would have to take the instructions of a servant girl in his household. Naaman was considered a great general in his hometown, and the king held him in the highest regard. Although he was considered a mighty man of valor, Naaman had an affliction of leprosy.

Like other great leaders, Naaman had a pride issue. He would have to humble himself to a young servant girl in order to start his journey to getting healed. 2 Kings 5:2-3 states, "At this time, Aramean raiders had invaded the land of Israel, and among their captives was a young girl who had been given to Naaman's wife as a maid. One day, the girl said to her mistress, 'I wish my master would go to see the prophet in Samaria. He would heal him of his leprosy.'"

Naaman was in a position where he wanted to get healed, so he would have to take the advice of the young servant girl. God tells us in Matthew 18:4, "So anyone who becomes as humble as this little child is the greatest in the Kingdom of Heaven. And anyone who welcomes a little child like this on my behalf is welcoming me." Later, we see that Naaman did have a pride issue. He went to the prophet Elisha, and Elisha sent a message that he should go wash in the Jordan seven times. Naaman was angry, because the prophet Elisha didn't come and tell him face-to-face. A messenger told him what to do. Naaman knew he had to humble himself after his officers reasoned with him, so he decided to give it a chance. It would take great humility on his part to dip himself seven times in the muddy waters of the Jordan.

This scenario involved a high official going down to the Jordan, and trusting that the water would heal him of leprosy. In many ways, we have to trust God in the same way. Sometimes, what we read in the Bible and what we are hearing in church does not line up with our thinking. In Proverbs 3:5, God tells us not to lean on our own thoughts and we know that God's ways and thoughts are far different than our thoughts.

Naaman was healed in the Jordan. We should think about what God has told us to do to solve a problem Like Naaman, sometimes we have to get in the muddy waters to be cleaned up by God.

#32: The Basin Principle

After that, he poured water into a basin and began to wash his disciple's
feet, drying them with the towel that was wrapped around him. He came
to Simon Peter, who said to him, "Lord, are you going to wash my feet?"
Jesus replied, "You do not realize now what I am doing, but later you will
understand." "No," said Peter, "you shall never wash my feet." Jesus answered,
"Unless I wash you, you have no part with me."
—John 13:5-8

Foot washing was a lowly service, and was normally performed by a servant. A basin was used for cleansing. Jesus performed the duty that, normally, a low servant would perform, but there He was, demonstrating humility to the disciples. He used a basin to perform a menial task, but Simon Peter showed his pride when Jesus was about to wash his feet. Simon did not want Jesus to perform such a low act of service on him. He actually wanted to wash Jesus' feet. Jesus instructed him that it had to be this way for now, and that he would understand it later. Jesus was preparing them for ministry, and the foot washing was a symbolic way of cleansing them for priesthood and discipleship. Jesus used his basin to serve the disciples.

In the book of Matthew, the basin was not used for service, but for washing hands. Matthew 27:22-24 states, "What shall I do, then, with Jesus who is called Christ?" Pilate asked. They all answered, "Crucify him!" "Why? What crime has he committed?" asked Pilate. But they shouted all the louder, "Crucify him!" When Pilate saw that he was getting nowhere, but that instead an uproar was starting, he took water and washed his hand in front of the crowd. "I am innocent of this man's blood, he said. "It is your responsibility!" Some translations said that he took a basin and washed his hands of the situation. Pride also got in the way of Pilate's decision-making. He was afraid of losing his position, and if he sided with Jesus, then he would be not in the people's favor. His pride caused him to just wash his hands of the situation, and he was too prideful to let Jesus go. By him not making a decision, he actually made the decision.

We don't have to have a basin to serve others, and if we dropped down and started washing people's feet today they would react like Simon Peter. Likewise, sometimes it's hard to have our feet washed because of pride. We don't want people to see our feet, or we have a sense of arrogance about someone bathing us. Pride wants us to be dependent on ourselves.

We can ask ourselves: what acts of service have we given to others? In what situations has pride led us to make a bad decision? Jesus later went through the most humbling thing that has ever been performed, and that was to die of an unrighteous death on the cross for our sins. He could not have done that with a prideful heart, and he died to give us salvation along with freedom from death. Jesus sets the ultimate leadership example, showing us the epitome of servanthood. What are we going to do with our basin? Do we even have water in our basin? Let's go wash some feet today. Let's let others wash our feet. We need to wash away the pride.

#33: Pride Starts With "I"

All this happened to King Nebuchadnezzar. Twelve months later, as the king was walking on the roof of the royal palace of Babylon, he said, "Is not this the great Babylon I have built as the royal residence, by my mighty power and for the glory of my majesty?" The words were still on his lips when a voice came from heaven, "This is what is decreed for you, King Nebuchadnezzar: Your royal authority has been taken from you. You will be driven away from people and will live with the wild animals; you will eat grass like cattle. Seven times will pass by for you until you acknowledge that the Most High is sovereign over the kingdoms of men and gives them to anyone he wishes."
—Daniel 4:28-32

In team sports, it takes a group effort in order to win a championship. No one person is bigger than the team, and the coach has to motivate the players to rally together as a team. Sometimes, a team will have a superstar or a player who is exceptional in a category who lets everyone know that he is the best. This type of player causes strife on the team. It comes down to pride. Pride exists in confrontation when a person starts a sentence with "I."

Proverbs 16:18 states, "Pride goes before destruction, a haughty spirit before a fall." Instead of giving God the credit for his success, Nebuchadnezzar took the credit. He was confronted before he finished praising himself, and God said that He would take him to a low place where he would become like an animal and grow claws. He lived in that situation for seven years before God restored him and he gave God the credit He deserves as the Almighty God. Isaiah 2:17 says, "Human pride will be humbled, and human arrogance will be brought down. Only the Lord will be exalted on that day of judgment."

Like King Nebuchadnezzar, pride usually starts when we fail to give God credit, and we begin to rely on our own strength. Pride can happen when things are going well, and we forget to worship God or recognize Him for our success. Pride can cause us to fail to admit our mistakes. Pride is a result of wanting attention. I am not saying that we should not celebrate success—we should be happy when God is doing great works through us. We just need to make sure that we are giving God the credit for what He is doing through our life.

As we go through each day, we need to examine areas in our life where we have been puffed up, and in what ways we are making unreasonable claims. We should think about what areas we need to ask God forgiveness for, and in what ways we can remain humble. It is easy to go from humility to prideful, and a thin line exists between the two. Sometimes, we want others to give us a pat on the back for an accomplishment. Other times, pride wants power. No matter what the circumstance, we just have to stop being self-focused for accomplishments and be more God-focused for our success.

#34: Demotion From Pride

When the men of Israel saw that their situation was critical and that their army was hard pressed, they hid in caves and thickets, among the rocks, and in pits and cisterns. Some Hebrews even crossed the Jordan to the land of Gad and Gilead. Saul remained at Gilgal, and all the troops with him were quaking with fear. He waited seven days, the time set by Samuel; but Samuel did not come to Gilgal, and Saul's men began to scatter. So he said, bring me the burnt offering and the fellowship offerings. And Saul offered up the burnt offering. Just as he finished making the offering, Samuel arrived, and Saul went out to greet him. "What have you done?" asked Samuel. Saul replied, "When I saw that the men were scattering, and that you did not come at the set time, and that the Philistines were assembling at Micmash, I thought, now the Philistines will come down against me at Gilgal, and I have not sought the Lord's favor. So I felt compelled to offer the burnt offering. But now your kingdom will not endure; the Lord has sought out a man after his own heart, and appointed him leader of his people, because you have not kept the Lord's command."
—1 Samuel 13:6-14

Many leaders get arrogant and feel that they can do their job better than their supervisors. Sometimes, it is hard leading from the middle of the pack, but boundaries exist. A coach may do things that are above the athletic director, or the athlete may put himself above the team. In some situations, this behavior can cause a job, a professional career, and sometimes it can be fatal. Without patience and obedience, a leader may react irrational, and do things that are not a part of his job description. Regardless, some of those things should not be done.

We can see how fear caused Saul to respond in a prideful way. He did something that only the prophet was supposed to do. He and his men became fearful, because Samuel had not arrived. His troops were starting to scatter, and it may have looked like they were losing the war. Like Adam and Eve taking the apple, Saul offered the burnt offering, which was not in his job description as king. This offering was only to be done by the priest. Because of his disobedience, he lost his role as king, and God appointed David, a man after his own heart. Saul was supposed to wait for Samuel to offer up the burnt offerings before going to battle, and Samuel was supposed to arrive in seven days. Saul's impatience and pride caused him the kingdom. They were not supposed to go to battle until the prophet Samuel offered the burnt offering. Samuel, like Moses who hit the rock twice, disobeyed God and he lost his kingdom role.

No matter how difficult the circumstances, we have to just trust God and hold on. Pressure may come from all angles, but we must wait on the Lord. In Isaiah 40:31, His word tells us that if we wait on Him, He will renew our strength. God is always just a prayer away, and we must not forego our blessings by doing things which are not God's will. Things of today that are similar to Saul's situation would be talking to sorcerers, shacking up, listening to others who are ungodly, acting out of selfishness, and doing things that are not in our job description. The best job description is the Holy Bible. It tells us how much weight we can handle, the salary, the duties, responsibilities, and what the cost of the job will be. We should follow the ultimate job description, and be careful not to do things that are not in God's will.

#35: Don't Let the Enemy's Pride Cause You to Stumble

Meanwhile, the Philistine, with his shield bearer in front of him, kept coming closer to David. He looked David over and saw that he was only a boy, ruddy and handsome, and he despised him. He said to David, "Am I a dog that you come at me with sticks?" And the Philistine cursed David by his gods. "Come here," he said, "and I'll give your flesh to the birds of the air and the beasts of the field."
—1 Samuel 17:41-44

Little David was about to get into the fight of his life. The enemy Goliath was trying to intimidate him, and he was cursing him just as a bully would do. David could have become fearful and responded sinfully to the attack of the giant. Goliath was a prideful giant who was over nine feet tall and was referred to as a champion. Everyone else was afraid to fight him, and he taunted the Israelite soldiers. David agreed to fight the giant, and he was laughed at by many. King Saul offered David the armor because he was too afraid to take on Goliath. The pride of Goliath caused the Israelite army to stumble. God's word says that "The fear of the Lord is the beginning of wisdom, and the knowledge of the Holy One is insight" (Proverbs 9:10). Goliath was not the Lord, but the people of Israel were making him out to be a lord at the time. But David took on the giant Goliath, and he defeated him.

Samuel 17:41 and 17:48 refer to the Philistine coming closer to David. He wanted to get closer so he could take David out. The enemy will try to draw you in, and then he will try to destroy you. We should rejoice when the enemy is close, however, because it gives us an opportunity to see his weak points. But we have to be cautious. David knew that he could be successful against the giant, because God had given him previous victories against lions and bears. In the same way, when we are facing the enemy, God wants us to remember our previous victories, and He will give us wisdom to succeed when we are being spiritually attacked.

Another great warrior was not able to handle the pressure of the enemy getting close, although he was successful in the end. In Judges 16, Sampson allowed Delilah to get close to him, but he was deceived. He almost lost everything, but God gave him his power back in the end. David used the enemy's closeness to his advantage. He was able to use his weapon, the slingshot. Likewise, God has given us weapons to deal with people who are difficult to get along with or people who are out to destroy us. We must use the sword (the Bible). Also, God encourages us to pray for those who persecute us. We need to be victorious, and not be trapped by the enemy's pride.

6

Prayer

#36: Instant Messaging

Jesus went out as usual to the Mount of Olives and his disciples followed him. On reaching the place, he said to them, "Pray that you will not fall into temptation." He withdrew about a stone's throw beyond them, knelt down, and prayed, "Father, if you are willing, take this cup from me; yet not my will, but yours be done."
—Luke 22:39-42

Individual prayer gives a person direct conversation with the Lord. When we made a phone call 50 years ago, we needed an operator to connect us to the person on the other line. Today, we have wireless phones, cell phones, instant messaging, and texting. We can find who we are looking for in a matter of seconds or at least get a message to that person. In certain religions and denominations, many believe that in order to reach God, we have to go through a priest or another person. After Christ died for our sins, He gave us direct access to God. He is the only way to God. Although the call may be wireless or instant messaging, Jesus is the mediator. In John 14:6-7, Jesus answered, "I am the way and the truth and the life. No one comes to the Father except through me. If you really knew me, you would know my Father as well. From now on, you do know him and have seen him." Although we are in a different time when everything is on speed dial, in order to reach God, we have to go through Jesus, and if we know Jesus, then we know God.

Luke 22:39 states that Jesus went out as usual to the Mount of Olives. Notice that God uses the word "usual." Usual means something that occurs all the time. Thus, the Mount of Olives was a praying place for Jesus all the time. We all should have a praying place, or a place where we can be in the presence in the Lord. The truth of the matter is that we can call on the Lord anywhere at any time. When His disciples were with him, Jesus asked them to pray that "they do not fall into temptation." In other words, while Jesus was praying, He specifically asked them to pray about temptation. This incident occurred during the season right before he was captured, and perhaps He knew that Peter and the other disciples would deny Him when He was arrested.

The Bible says that Jesus withdrew about a stone's throw away from the other disciples. Why would He move away from the disciples to pray? We all need our own private time with God. Jesus had just instructed the disciples to pray that they would not fall into temptation. Countless times, He led them in prayer, but this one time He needed to go to God individually. This pattern teaches us that it is important to be alone with God and pray. Jesus teaches us the way in this illustration. The following is an important prayer, because Jesus asked God to take the cup off of him, but He clearly stated that He would do the will of God. Luke 22:42 reads, "Father, If you are willing, take this cup from me; yet not my will, but yours be done." Although Jesus could have been selfish, He put the decision back on God, and He finished by saying "the Father's will be done." He is ready to bear our sins no matter the consequences and pain.

We need to think about where our prayer life is today and be able to get alone with God. We shouldn't duck the tests and trials that God is putting us through to reshape us more to be like Him. Jesus took the cup for us. Now, we need to take the cup for Him. It is not our will be done, rather, it is the Father's will be done.

#37: Sweat Blood

An angel from heaven appeared to him and strengthened him. And being in anguish, he prayed more earnestly and his sweat was like drops of blood falling to the ground. When he rose from prayer and went back to the disciples, he found them asleep, exhausted from sorrow. He said, "Get up and pray so that you will not fall into temptation."
—Luke 22:43-46

Back in the mid 1990s, I had the wonderful experience of working with and assisting the Virginia Tech football team in the weight room. I received such great leadership from Coach Mike Gentry, who is still leading the team in strength and conditioning, and he has been noted for part of the success of the team over the last decade. Coach Gentry was great with motivating the players and he was also great with motivating his staff members. Coach Gentry used to give the players shirts with motivating quotes and sayings. One of the shirts read, "Sweat Blood." Now, that is intense sweating! In other words, a player needs to be working so hard that they are sweating blood through their pores, which is realistically possible. If the body is under such great stress, it is physically possible to bring blood up through the pores. Most coaches want to put a lot of stress on athletes' bodies, because what does not kill them will make them stronger and the muscles will adapt and grow back stronger than ever.

Right before Jesus was arrested, He was under great stress. He knew that He had to take on one of the most painful deaths in order to save mankind from eternal death. But we are not alone, no matter what we are facing. Luke 22:43 states that an angel came and strengthened Jesus during this time of prayer. Like Jesus, when we are in prayer and trusting God to get through an illness or a tough situation, He comforts us with his angels. In that verse, it states that He was in anguish. Anguish means that He was in extreme pain and intense suffering. Before the crucifixion even started, Jesus started to feel what was about to happen. But He kept on praying earnestly, and He continued to rely on God. Also, in that passage, it says that Jesus prayed more earnestly, meaning that He took His prayer to another level. We have to do the same thing when trials and suffering come. We have to step up our prayer life, and we need to pray with intensity and focus. So often, we pray right before bedtime, but we fall asleep before even finishing the prayer. When we are in anguish like Jesus, we need to step up our prayer life. Jesus warns that without prayer, we can fall into temptation.

The thing that gets our attention in this instance is that He is praying so intensely and earnestly that He is sweating blood. Many doubt whether He was actually sweating blood, but Luke, the physician and disciple, gave a description of what he witnessed. Like the football players who need to make physical adaptations to win, Jesus is setting an example here of how we need to pray until sweat is dripping off of us, which means that our prayer life needs to be serious and focused. The football players get stronger through physical training and practice, and we get stronger through intense and earnest prayer.

The disciples were sleeping when Jesus got up from prayer. Jesus warned of falling into temptation. The guards were upon Jesus as He was telling them to get up and pray so that they would not fall into temptation. We need to pray intensely and with deep emotion. We need to sweat blood.

#38: MRE

*Evening, morning, and at noon, I will pray, and cry aloud,
and He shall hear my voice.*
—Psalm 55:17

A short period existed in my life where I planned to go in the military, and I learned about MREs. When you are out on a mountainside or in a foxhole, you may not have a nice, hot dinner every day or even for weeks. Many times, military personnel are dug in for days without having a traditional meal to eat. That's why they rely on MREs, which are "meals ready to eat." The meals are somewhat compressed, but they come in little square packages that remain preserved, no matter what the temperature is outside. After trying one of these meals, I felt sick to my stomach and wondered how in the world anyone could survive on this stuff. I wondered how anyone could eat a mimicked meal for many days. When someone's life is on the line, taste is not an issue. The soldier, at that point, is eating for life and not for taste.

Our prayer life is similar to the MREs. We need to have them during the times when we are in a foxhole, and we don't know how things are going to turn out. Times may exist when the collectors or the banks are calling, and other times where we don't know which way to turn. Although the finances and food may be scarce, a higher strength always exists that we can rely on and that is Jesus Christ. Matthew 11:28-30 states, "Come to me, all you who are weary and burdened, and I will give you rest. Take my yoke upon you and learn from me, for I am gentle and humble in heart, and you will find rest for your souls. For my yoke is easy and my burden is light." Jesus has something way better than the MREs. When in times of distress, He wants us to pray. He wants us to bring all of our burdens to Him. He is telling us that His way is a lot lighter than our way.

In Psalm 55:17 God is showing us how He wants us to pray. The passage states, "Evening, and morning, and at noon, I will pray, and cry aloud: and he shall hear my voice." God is not so concerned with how long we pray or how many times we pray, but His word lets us know that we do need to pray. When a military soldier is feeling starved and empty, he still has the MREs to turn to. Although it may not be what he wants to eat at the time, it still keeps him alive and gets him through the tough times. Our prayer life is the same way. We often eat three hot meals a day, and God is telling us in Psalm 55:17 that we need to pray evening, morning, and at noon. Ironically, the times line up with meal times. People often say that they don't have time to pray, but we can always cry out to the Lord during meal time, which is a minimum of three times a day. As the MREs nourish our body, the prayers will nourish our body and our spiritual soul as well. Prayer will lift the burdens of life off of us.

Just as Daniel went into his chamber and prayed three times a day, it would be beneficial for us to pray multiple times a day as well. No matter how we do it, we know that like the soldier who needs MREs during the desert experiences, we need prayer during the valley experiences and everyday experiences.

We need to think about how we can become more devoted to talking to God, and how we can increase our prayer life. It is through the prayer life that we develop a greater relationship with Jesus Christ, and it is through prayer that we are fed. It is said that physical training is of value, but spiritual training is of more value. We have to train the spiritual being by incorporating prayer into our daily routine. We need to make a renewed commitment to pray more consistently to God. His comfort is our MRE, and we need to call upon him during our foxhole experiences.

#39: Don't Worry, Be Happy

Be joyful always, pray continually, give thanks in all circumstances,
for this is God's will for you in Christ Jesus.
—1 Thessalonians 5:16

I remember a song called "Don't Worry, Be Happy." The music video pictured an artist who was happy no matter what was going on around him. You can go to a local airport and if you look at people's eyes, they are not happy. In today's time, very few people greet others with a smile. The Bible states in Proverbs 17:22, "A cheerful heart is good medicine, but a crushed spirit dries up the bones." Smiling is good energy. One thing is for sure—very few people have heart attacks while laughing. Statistics even show that laughter may prevent a heart attack.

In 1 Thessalonians 5:16, God tells us to be joyful always. We can't change our attitude based on what is happening in our life. We need to smile in the good times and the bad times. Worry can lead us into sin, because we stop trusting God and we lean on our own strength. God encourages us by showing that we are His children, and that He will take care of us just as He takes care of the birds of the air. Matthew 6:25-29 says, "Therefore I tell you, do not worry about your life, what you will eat or drink; or about your body, what you will wear. Is not life more important than food, and the body more important than clothes? Look at the birds of the air; they do not sow or reap or store away in barns, and yet your heavenly Father feeds them. Are you not much more valuable than they? Who of you by worrying can add a single hour to his life? And why do you worry about clothes? See how the lilies of the field grow. They do not labor or spin. Yet I tell you that not even Solomon in all his splendor was dressed like one of these."

We might as well be joyful, and continue to believe and trust in God. In the previous passage, God clearly shows us that He will give us the basic necessities we need to survive. We should be happy always, because of what Christ has done in our life.

In 1 Thessalonians 5:16, God also tells us to pray continually. Our human nature only reaches and cries out to God during the tough times. God wants to hear from us on a daily basis. He is only a prayer away. Through prayer, we are able to increase our faith, love, and endurance inspired by hope. Prayer brings joy in itself. We should go to God not only to ask for things in prayer, but first and foremost to just recognize and praise God for being the Creator. We should praise Him for giving us His only begotten Son Jesus Christ, who died for our sins on the cross. Prayer increases faith, and prayer increases our joy. In Romans 1:9-10, Paul also shows a pattern and blueprint in how often we should pray. The passage says, "God, whom I serve with my whole heart in preaching the gospel of His Son, is my witness how constantly I remember you in my prayers at all times; and I pray that now at last by God's will the way may be opened for me to come to you." The bottom line is that we need to consistently go to the Lord in prayer, and we can give praise, intercede for others who are not praying for themselves, and pray so that we will not fall into temptation. During prayer, we need to give God thanks in all circumstances as He instructs us in His word.

#40: The Food Guide—Three Prayers a Day

*Now when Daniel learned that the decree had been published, he
went home to his upstairs room where the windows opened
toward Jerusalem. Three times a day he got down on his knees
and prayed, giving thanks to his God, just as he had done before.
Then these men went as a group and found Daniel praying and
asking God for help. So they went to the king and spoke to him
about his royal decree: "Did you not publish a decree that during
the next thirty days anyone who prays to any god or man except
to you, O king, would be thrown into the lions' den?" The king
answered, "The decree stands—in accordance with the laws of the
Medes and Persians, which cannot be repealed."*
—Daniel 6:10-12

Modern times are very similar to the Biblical times of Daniel. In public school systems, teachers and students who pray to God can be persecuted. In the workplace, people have to be careful about having anything of faith posted in their work area, such as Bible verses and e-mails with scriptures attached in the signature area. Leaders can lose their jobs or be judged harshly by others for openly expressing their faith. Nothing has really changed today as compared to what Daniel faced thousands of years ago.

Daniel was a prayer warrior, and he set the example for praying. Daniel 6:10 says that Daniel routinely prayed three times a day in his upper room. But Daniel, because of his high position, was unaware that some of the men were trying to find fault in him so he would lose his high position. They found Daniel praying in the upper room, and little did Daniel know that the men had the king publish a decree saying that everyone should pray to the king in that 30-day period. The men reported to the King that Daniel was praying. Daniel did not hide his prayer life, because the Bible states that the place he prayed opened up toward Jerusalem. Daniel, who denied the royal food earlier, was going against the grain by praying to God. The men reported him, and Daniel would have to face the lion's den by not obeying the decree. Daniel continued to pray, even if it meant that he would be put to death.

Although Daniel was thrown in the lion's den for praying, the lion's did not attack him—his prayer saved him. The king that ordered him to be thrown in the lion's den also encouraged Daniel and respected the almighty God. Daniel 6:16 says, "May your God, whom you serve continually rescue you!" Although he was sentencing Daniel to a death sentence, he still wished him well. The lions would not eat Daniel. The many prayer meals before being placed in the den protected him. Surely, he turned the prayer volume and intensity up while he was in the den. The people who plotted against Daniel ended up being tossed in the lion's den by the order of the king and they were eaten by the lions.

Prayer protects us from our foes and when we are in the lion dens of life. We may not pray three times a day like Daniel, but we just need to pray. We need to get on our hands and knees and draw from God the same power and protection that Daniel received. We need to give God thanks today for prayer.

#41: The 21-Day Fast and Prayer

At that time I, Daniel, mourned, for three weeks. I ate no choice food; no meat or wine touched my lips; and I used no lotions at all until the three weeks were over. On the twenty-fourth day of the first month, as I was standing on the bank of the great river, the Tigris, I looked up and there before me was a man dressed in linen, with a belt of the finest gold around his waist.
—Daniel 10:2-5

In a ball game, it is easy to get impatient, and make quick, harsh decisions. Sometimes, baseball coaches pull their ace pitcher too soon or a lineman in football jumps offsides before the snap starts. Many times, people give up in the middle of their career, because they are not being promoted fast enough. Many people want instant success, and they don't want to wait on God. I remember a time in my life when I didn't hear from God soon enough, and I ran ahead of Him and did things in my flesh and leaned on my own understanding.

Consider the Bible story of Abraham and Sarah. They were both well in age, and God had promised them that they would have children as numerous as the stars. Before this promise would happen, they ran ahead of God, and Sarah gave one of her maidservants to her husband so they could have a family. This incident was one of the first forms of adultery, and it caused a broken home.

One thing that gives us clarity in decision-making and patience is fasting and prayer. God shows up somewhere during or after the period of prayer and fasting. Daniel demonstrated the importance of fasting and praying together, and he showed us perseverance. In Daniel 10:2, the Bible states that he mourned for three weeks. He denied his body of desired foods. Daniel had been victorious before with God when he fasted for 10 days, and his body appeared healthier than those who ate the royal food. Daniel would win again in the lion's den, and perhaps his dedication of praying three times a day covered him later in the fiery furnace. Daniel had been waiting on a message from God for 21 days, and Daniel 10:4 states that the message didn't come until the 24th day. Daniel could have given up after 21 days, but he had seen God come through on previous occasions. An angel was sent on the 24th day, and the angel brought him a message. The Bible talks about how the messenger was held up, which lets us know that the enemy will try to block our blessings. We fight against flesh and blood, but also against evil forces.

As the stakes of life get higher, we need a more consistent prayer life. The bigger the issues we face, the more prayer is needed. The bigger the issues of life, the more fasting and prayer are needed. Daniel was fatigued and tired when the angels brought him the message and vision. Once the vision did arrive, Daniel still had enough strength to deliver the message. He saw the vision, and others didn't see what he saw. Likewise, in today's world, family, coworkers, and others may not see what you see. They give up, and go on with other paths of life while you continue to hold on. God meant for Daniel to see the angel, and others were feared by what Daniel had seen. When we tell people what we see, they sometimes become scared and withdraw. They give up on us or they are not willing to make the journey. It would be typical to fast three weeks, and then go back to the natural flow of life. On the 24th day, God showed up and showed off. Daniel would get his message not in his time, but he would get it in his timing. We need to think about the things in our life that we trust God for. We need to pray and fast for an answer.

#42: The Lord's Prayer

*Our Father in heaven, hallowed be your name, your kingdom come, your will
be done on earth as it is in heaven. Give us today our daily bread. Forgive us our
debts, as we also have forgiven our debtors. And lead us not into temptation,
but deliver us from the evil one. For if you forgive men when they sin against you,
your heavenly Father will also forgive you. But if you do not forgive
men their sins, your Father will not forgive your sins.*
—Matthew 6:9-15

Many athletic teams incorporate the Lord's Prayer in their pregame routine and in after-game victories. When I was the strength and conditioning coach at a school years ago, we always said the prayer after games, no matter what the turnout. We started incorporating the prayer after practices. It is a powerful prayer to pray. Sometimes, if you rehearse something too much, you may forget the meaning behind it. The words just become common words, and it just becomes an expression of speech. We forget the power in the words, and the prayer loses its significant power. In sports, we sometimes say that you have to have mind, body, and spirit. When we deeply cherish each word of the Bible and the Lord's spirit, the words become more than a slur of speech.

The first part of the verse in Matthew 6:9 says, "Our Father in heaven, hallowed be your name, your kingdom come, your will be done on earth as it is in heaven." This message teaches all of us in prayer to first recognize God, and praise Him for the kingdom He created. We also must first say, "your will be done," no matter what we may be trusting God to do in our life. We may want the Lord to bless us with finances, restore a relationship, and/or ask God to meet other peoples' needs. But first, we must hallow His name in praise and worship, and no matter how big our desires, His will be done. At this point, it gets tough. Although we say to God, "your will be done," we get angry and upset when God does not meet our expectations. Jesus laid the pattern for all of us when He asked God to take the cup away from Him or pass His suffering. As in Luke 22:42, Jesus said, "not my will, but your will be done."

Before the Lord's Prayer, Matthew 6:8 states, "Do not be like them, for your Father knows what you need before you ask Him." That statement is so powerful! Although God knows what we need, we still need to go to Him to prayer and ask. We have to keep the lines of communication open with God. He wants us to communicate, and build a deeper relationship with Him.

The Lord's Prayer says, "Give us this day our daily bread." We must be thankful for this day, and focus all of our time and energy on today, as tomorrow will have enough worries of its own. "Forgive us our debts, as we also have forgiven our debtors." Debt is not merely a financial thing. The debt is our weighed down sin. Jesus forgave us, so we must forgive those who sin against us. "And lead us not into temptation, but deliver us from the evil one." We must be diligent in prayer asking God to strengthen us, like He did for Jesus when He was being tempted by Satan. Ephesians 6:11 says, we must also put on God's armor daily to protect ourselves from the enemy. The last part of the Lord's Prayer says, "We must truly forgive those who have sinned against us, or the Lord will not forgive us of our shortcomings."

When people hurt us or take advantage of us, we don't want to forgive them, which actually forfeits our opportunity to be with God. We must dig deep down, and forgive the person. When we don't forgive, we can't move forward, which keeps a hidden anger. We need to think about who we need to forgive in prayer.

7

Vision and Dreams

#43: Focus Brings Vision

Where there is no prophecy, the people cast off restraint,
but happy are those who keep the law.
—Proverbs 29:18

Other translations of Proverbs 29:18 have said that people with no vision need to cast off restraint, but happy is he who keeps the law. Merriam-Webster defines vision as something seen otherwise than by ordinary sight, a vivid picture created by the imagination, or an unusual wisdom in foreseeing what is going to happen. Vision is the act or power of seeing. Many see that prophecy as being a priest, preacher, or a prophet who cast the vision for people.

Baseball and softball players must have exceptional vision. A batter has a split second to decide whether he will swing at the hurled baseball. He must be able to discern whether the pitch is a fastball or curveball. The outfield must be able to judge the location of a fly ball as it leaves the bat. An outfielder who misjudges a long fly ball may cause his team to lose. Likewise, a batter who can't hit a breaking pitch is considered to have poor vision. In the movie *Major League*, the pitcher was not able to throw strikes until he got prescription glasses. He could not focus on where he needed to throw the ball without the glasses, but once he received his glasses he was a better pitcher.

Focus is the key to vision. We need to think about what we are focusing on. For example, think of the lenses on an overhead projector. Without getting the lenses in focus, we will not be able to see what we are looking for. Light can bring a better vision. The lights in a room can be dimmed during a presentation, which will put more focus on the light coming from the projector. Another translation of Proverbs 29:18 states, "where there is no vision, the people will perish," which is why it is so important for the pastor or leader to have good vision. He must be focused on Jesus Christ, the author and finisher of our faith. The pastor must cast the vision, and the vision in itself is a focus on Jesus Christ. When the pastor is focused on Jesus, he directs the people of the congregation to also focus on Jesus. It is crucial that all leaders have their focus on God. Otherwise, they could cause others to stumble. They have to stay focused at all times.

The second part of the passage says, "Happy is he who keeps the law." The leader who keeps the law will be happy, and he will be able to cast vision as long as he is focused on Christ. He will be able to shed the vision of Christ to others, and through this vision the leader will be able to prevent others from perishing. The vision is for the leader to focus on Jesus Christ, and by sharing the vision with others, the goal is to help them become more focused and to prevent any souls from perishing.

#44: Dreams Deferred

Now Joseph had a dream, and he told it to his brothers; and they hated him even more. So he said to them, "Please hear this dream which I have dreamed: There we were, binding sheaves in the field. Then behold, my sheaf arose and also stood upright; and indeed your sheaves stood all around and bowed down to my sheaf."
—Genesis 37:5-7

Now when they saw him afar off, even before he came near them, they conspired against him to kill him. Then they said to one another, "Look, this dreamer is coming! Come therefore, let us now kill him and cast him into some pit; and we shall say, 'Some wild beast has devoured him.' We shall see what will become of his dreams!"
—Genesis 38:18-20

We have to learn from Joseph. You can't tell your dreams to everybody. God hears our dreams, but the devil also hears our dreams when we pray. In Genesis 37:5-7, Joseph shares his dreams with his brothers, and the Bible says that they hated him even more. We know that all things happen for the good of God. What could have been bad for Joseph actually turned into good. Joseph ended up becoming a major leader in the lands, and his brothers had to bow to him. Often in the workplace, people come against one another because of jealousy. We have to be careful with how much of our dreams and visions we share with others. People will not believe in us, especially if we are progressing toward our dreams.

Later, Joseph's brothers saw him from afar, and they planned to kill him. Instead, they threw their own brother in the pit. Joseph ended up in the pit for the same reason he got out of the pit. His dreams caused his brothers to envy him and turn against him. Later, while in prison, Joseph was directed into what his purpose was. He had to be in a low place, since he had also been falsely accused by Potiphar's wife. He had been hurt by his brothers and Potiphar's wife said that Joseph tried to be intimate with her. But while Joseph was in a capsized place, he interpreted dreams for the cup-bearer and the baker. Later, the cup-bearer was in the presence of the king, and the king had a dream that no one could interpret. The cup-bearer remembered what Joseph did for him, which he shared with the king. Joseph interpreted the king's dream, and the king put him in a high position. Joseph, through serving others and continuing to practice what he was good at, saw his dreams fulfilled.

We all have visions and dreams and we have to be like Joseph. Although we may be in a dark place in life, we have to continue to hope. We may not know what the future holds, but we need to use our talents on a lower level, and then someday we will be using our talents on the highest level. We need to brush off our dreams and start serving God and others, patterning the life of Jesus Christ.

#45: Now You See It, Now You Don't

Therefore we do not lose heart. Though outwardly we are wasting away, yet inwardly we are being renewed day by day. For our light and momentary troubles are achieving for us an eternal glory that far outweighs them all. So we fix our eyes not on what is seen, but on what is unseen. For what is seen is temporary, but what is unseen is eternal.
—2 Corinthians 4:16-18

Growing up as a kid, I had a fear of thunder and lightning. My grandmother always said, "Get away from the windows and everyone ready your Bible and pray." That strategy worked every time. I remember the first time that my mother dropped me off at Virginia Tech to attend the student transition program for minority students. A very serious thunderstorm came up that evening, but I remembered what my grandmother had told me to do many years ago, and I got my Bible and moved away from the window. We should never lose heart, no matter what the situation looks like on the outside, because eventually the storm will pass over.

2 Corinthians 4:16 tells us not to lose heart. Remember the Israelites who escaped Egypt that Moses led into the wilderness. They looked back and the Egyptians were quickly catching up to them. They must have felt overwhelmed by the army of Egyptians. But God made a way for the Israelites to pass through the Red Sea, and the Egyptians were swept away in the sea when they tried to pursue the Israelites. The second part of this verse states "though outwardly we are wasting away, yet inwardly we are being renewed day by day." When Abraham and Sarah looked worn out on the outside, God strengthened them internally and spiritually to birth a child in an impossible age.

Jesus went through a slight momentary affliction that prepared all mankind for eternity. 2 Corinthians 4:17 states, "For our light and momentary troubles are achieving for us an eternal glory that far outweighs them all." Jesus had a vision stronger than any other man. He tolerated affliction, slander, being spit on, and beaten, to a point where He was crucified for us. Jesus knew that he had to suffer for a crime that he didn't commit. By bearing our sins on the cross, He gave us eternal salvation as long as people believe in Him.

Finally, 2 Corinthian 4:18 states, "So we fix our eyes not on what is seen, but on what is unseen. For what is seen is temporary, but what is unseen is eternal." The Israelites who had first escaped Egypt were affirmed by God that they would receive the promised lands. When they went in to investigate the land, some of the spies were afraid of the giants in the land. God had already promised them the land, but the Israelites of that time focused on the temporary. Later, Joshua led the Israelites across the Jordan. Although the giants were still in the land, Joshua focused on what God had promised eternally.

When we are in the midst of a storm, we have to remember what God has said in His word. Jeremiah 29:11 says, "For I know the plans I have for you," declares the Lord, "plans to prosper you and not to harm you, plans to give you hope and a future."

#46: Turn On Your Heart Lights

The eye is the lamp of the body. If your eyes are good, your whole body will be full of light. But if your eyes are bad, your whole body will be full of darkness. If then, the light within you is darkness, how great is that darkness! No one can serve two masters. Either he will hate the one and love the other, or he will be devoted to the one and despise the other. You cannot serve both God and money.
—Matthew 6:22-24

During the production of a play, the light crew can put different shades of slides in front of the light lamps, which project different colors on the stage. It is a phenomenal sight for the audience, and it is a way of highlighting the actors on the stage. If we look at the lamps as being eyes, the slides put in front of the lamps project what we are looking at. Thus, the lamps are shining the color of the light that is in front of the lamp. If we have a yellow light in front of the lamp lenses, then the lamp will project yellow light. If a clear slide is in front of the lamp, then the lamp will reveal white light. The light that is projected is determined by what is put in front of the eyes of the lamp. Our body operates in the same fashion.

Matthew 6:22 states, "The eye is the lamp of the body. If your eyes are good, your whole body will be full of light." In the body, the light reflected from a person starts in his heart. But the Bible says that the eye is the lamp of the body. The eyes are actually the slides in front of our heart, because the light starts in our heart. If we have darkness in our heart, then our eyes will look at dark things and our spirit will reveal darkness. If the heart is full of light, then the eyes will look at things that are of light and the heart will reveal light.

Ephesians 1:18 says, "I pray also that the eyes of your heart may be enlightened in order that you may know the hope to which He has called you, the riches of the glorious inheritance in the saints." God refers to the eyes of the heart, and states that they may be enlightened. Therefore, in reality we have a hidden set of eyes in our hearts, and if they are enlightened, the bodily eyes will be enlightened. We know this factor is true from Matthew 6:23, which states, "if your eyes are bad, your whole body will be full of darkness."

The heart can't have both darkness and light. If the heart is yearning for sin, then the eyes will draw to it. It all starts in the heart. Matthew 5:28 says, "But I tell you that anyone who looks at a woman lustfully has already committed adultery with her in his heart." Matthew 6:24 states that we can't have two masters. The contrast is made between God and money. We will love one, and hate the other. Greed starts in the heart, and the outward actions of our use of money will reveal whether we love the Lord or not.

In order to control our eyes, we have to control our heart. It starts with God. As we draw closer to God, he will cleanse our heart. Like King David, we can ask God to give us a clean heart. Psalm 51:10 states, "Create in me a pure heart, O God, and renew a steadfast spirit within me." This plea is asking God to cleanse us from our sin, so we will have only bright light pouring from our heart. Our eyes will be fixed on the prize, and we will be champions for Christ. We need to think about what we are focusing on and identify the color of the lenses in front of our heart, whether it be light or darkness deep down in our heart.

#47: Don't Look Back, Look Up

*I will be careful to live a blameless life—I will lead a life of integrity
in my own home. I will refuse to look at anything vile and vulgar. I
hate all who deal crookedly; I will have nothing to do with them.*
—Psalm 101:2-3

What we look at today will affect us tomorrow. If we are reading today, then that will influence our leadership for tomorrow. What we allow to come through our eyes directly affects who we are inside. We all make a decision on what we will look upon, especially when no one is looking. Psalm 121:1-2 says, "I will lift up my eyes to the hills—from whence comes my help? My help comes from the Lord, Who made heaven and earth." We need to continue looking up to the Lord, which is truly where our strength and hope come from. In order to move closer to our dreams and aspirations, we also need to check our character. God can only do His part, but we have to do our part. Psalm 101:2-3 states that God encourages us to live a blameless life, and also our home life must reflect our character.

It all starts with our vision and eyes. We need to examine what we are looking at. Matthew 5:27-29 states, "You have heard that it was said to those of old, 'You shall not commit adultery.' But I say to you that whoever looks at a woman to lust for her has already committed adultery with her in his heart. If your right eye causes you to sin, pluck it out and cast it from you; for it is more profitable for you that one of your members perish, than for your whole body to be cast into hell." We have to be careful what we look at. We have to be careful where we allow our eyes to go, which can distort our vision and dreams. With the Internet and television, it is easy to get pulled into a world of sin. Although it may seem okay to look at a television show, we have to be careful because of the images that may prevail.

God often rescues us from sinful things. Remember the time of Abraham, Lot, and his wife. They were all rescued from Sodom and Gomorrah moments before God destroyed the town, because of the sin in the town. Genesis 19:23-26 states, "The sun had risen upon the earth when Lot entered Zoar. Then the Lord rained brimstone and fire on Sodom and Gomorrah, from the Lord out of the heavens. So He overthrew those cities, all the plain, all the inhabitants of the cities, and what grew on the ground. But his wife looked back behind him, and she became a pillar of salt."

When leaving a sinful situation, we should not look back. Lot's wife, who perhaps was still yearning for the days in Sodom and Gomorrah, looked back after the angels had told her not to look back as the city was being destroyed and she turned into a pillar of salt. Philippians 3:13-14 states, "Not that I have already attained, or am already perfected; but I press on, that I may lay hold of that for which Christ Jesus has also laid hold of me. Brethren, I do not count myself to have apprehended; but one thing I do, forgetting those things which are behind and reaching forward to those things which are ahead, I press toward the goal for the prize of the upward call of God in Christ Jesus."

What things do we need to forget about, and what things do we need to stop viewing that may not be pleasing to God? We should keep our eyes in the front-view mirror, and limit our time looking in the rearview mirror. Hebrews 12:2 says, "Let's fix our eyes on Jesus, the author and finisher of our faith."

#48: I Have the Vision

"In the last days," God says, "I will pour out my Spirit on all people. Your sons and daughters will prophesy, your young men will see visions, your old men will dream dreams. Even on my servants, both men and women, I will pour out my spirit in those days, and they will prophesy. I will show wonders in the heaven above and signs on the earth below, blood and fire and bills of smoke."
—Acts 2:17-19

Every person is not born with good physical sight. They may have to wear glasses, contacts, or even have surgery in order to have 20/20 vision. Some people have good vision in one eye, but they have trouble seeing in the other eye. If you have ever been lost, you are often looking for an object or a certain landscape that lets you know if you are in the vicinity of where you want to go. I remember driving across the desert in Arizona to the Grand Canyon. I had heard about and seen images of the wonderful sight, and I could not wait to get there. As I drove across the desert plains, I felt as if I was not going in the right direction, but things began to change. The landscape became more rocky and hilly along the way. I started seeing Indian reservations, and the mountains began to soar above the horizon. I knew something great was up ahead. I had hope that I was on the right trail, and I drove ahead with boldness and confidence.

God gives us a powerful vision, and that vision comes through the Holy Spirit. Before the vision came, we were lost. Jesus left us with a guide, and this guide helps us when we have no direction in life. In Acts 2:17, God clearly states that this vision is available to all people, and it has been provided for all people. Jesus left us a comforter, and through this comforter we have Christ-like vision and power. We are able to do things that we didn't think we could do. This Holy Spirit is poured out on us, and we just have to be open to receive the vision.

The young and old will be able to proclaim the good news. God is letting us know that the vision is not just for the young, but it is also for the old. If someone is dreaming, then that means that the possibility of something happening exists. Sometimes people get to a certain age, and they start looking back on their life thinking about all the things they wish they had done. People are not sad that they are at a ripe old age and about to die; people are sad because they never lived. God says that old men will dream dreams. The young need direction and that direction comes from God. God says that young men will be given a vision. A vision gives direction along the pathways of life. A young person may not know what college to attend, or he may not know what team to join. God already knows the past, present, and future, so no one is better to turn to. We need to talk to God about our future.

When we see wonders like the Grand Canyon, it is a sign that God exists and that we are headed in the right direction. We need our GPS system—the Holy Spirit—which gives direction and a life compass.

8

Holy Spirit

#49: The Spirit of Truth vs. the Spirit of Falsehood

You, dear children, are from God and have overcome them,
because the one who is in you is greater than the one who is in
the world. They are from the world and therefore speak from the
viewpoint of the world, and the world listens to them. We are from
God, and whoever knows God listens to us; but whoever is not
from God does not listen to us. This is how we recognize the Spirit
of truth and the spirit of falsehood.
—1 John 4:4-6

When we accept Jesus as our Lord and Savior, we become children of God. Matthew 18:3 reads, "And he said: 'I tell you the truth, unless you change and become like little children, you will never enter the kingdom of God.'" It is very important that we train children in the way that they should go, and they will never turn away from it. Proverbs 22:6 explains this verse. It states, "Train a child in the way he should go, and when he is old he will not turn from it." Once a person accepts Christ as his Lord and Savior, he becomes a part of the winning team. Jesus is the coach of our team, and of course the first string was the disciples. The great thing about being on Jesus' team is that we are able to tap into some of his resurrection power. As Christians, we are able to pray for others, rebuke the enemy, provide healing, and provide hope. We can increase the faith of others by sharing the gospel, and winning others to the best team ever.

1 John 4:4 states, "…and have overcome them, because the one who is in you is greater than the one who is in the world." "Them" can represent those who are not on the team or those who are of the evil spirit, the devil. The "world" refers to people who live their lives for now. Those who know Jesus Christ as their Lord and Savior already have the victory and have more power than those in the world. Whether you are in sports, sales, or another leadership capacity, the victory is in these words. We have something greater in us than the world can offer. We have to remember that power every day. We already have what it takes to win at any endeavor; we just need to get everyone on the team to continue to believe in this higher power that exists in the soul. That power is the Holy Spirit, and it is the Spirit of God. It is similar to the power that Jesus used to do wonder when He was walking the earth.

The opposing team has different attitudes, differs in all facets, and has no love for those who have the Holy Spirit. Throughout the heat of competition, the opposing team will make every attempt to bring fear into those who have the Holy Spirit.

God gives us a sign of who will make great teammates. God also indicates how we will recognize those who are for us. They will have the spirit of truth. This spirit of truth is the Holy Spirit, which is given by grace by God. Teammates are going to bring the spirit of truth to the team, which includes love, joy, peace, patience, kindness, goodness, faithfulness, gentleness, and self-control. The spirit of falsehood opposes the "fruit of the spirit" referred to in Galatians 5:22. If we are faced with anger, hatred, opposing forces, pride, vanity, and anything that is contrary to the will of God is of the evil one. This evil spirit entered the serpent and deceived Eve. This evil spirit entered Judas Iscariot, making him deceive Jesus. Jesus has resurrection power, and He overcame death, which gives us Christ-like power. We have something deep within us that can fight any battle or opposition that comes our way.

#50: The Counselor

And I will ask the Father, and he will give you another Counselor to be with you forever—the Spirit of truth. The world cannot accept him, because it neither sees him nor knows him. But you know him, for he lives with you and will be in you. I will not leave you as orphans; I will come to you. Before long, the world will not see me anymore, but you will see me. Because I live, you also will live.
—John 14:16-18

A counselor is someone who gives hope or provides help. The Bible speaks of getting wise counsel when we are under distress. When we go to the Lord in prayer, no wiser counselor exists than praying to God himself. But we know that we must pray, keeping Jesus in mind, and we know that the Spirit of truth (Holy Spirit) lives within us. In John 14:6, Jesus answered, "I am the way and the truth and the life. No one comes to the Father except through me." Jesus is our counselor, and through the Spirit of truth we receive some of the same powers that lifted Jesus from death on the third day. We are also equipped with some of the same powers that can heal, and that can rebuke evil spirits.

Jesus definitely didn't abandon us when he left the earth. He left a part of His glory with us, and that is the Spirit of truth, which resides in us to give us comfort. The first sign of this Holy Spirit was at the day of Pentecost. Acts 2:4 states, "All of them were filled with the Holy Spirit and now began to speak in other tongues as the Spirit enabled them."

The world does not have this Spirit of truth. People who do not accept Jesus as the Son of God live by the world's terms, which means they store up earthly possessions, live for today, and do not consider eternity. Some people may feel that they are good people, and don't have to read scripture or have a relationship with God. It is not about how many hours we spend at church; it is about having a relationship with God through prayer, and following the Spirit of truth that resides in us as believers in Jesus Christ. Some people may ask, "How do we know that all this exists, or what if we live righteous and no God exists?" Our lives are no bigger than a pencil dot on a sheet of paper. The paper itself is eternity. We are only here for a short while, and we have to know that God has something better for us in heaven. We won't have to endure anymore suffering, pain, personal attacks, final struggles, sickness, or wrongdoing.

God reveals to us that although we can't see him, he does exist. In 1 Corinthians 2:9 God reveals the unknown. The passage states, "No eye has seen, no ear has heard, no man has conceived what God has prepared for those who love him." But God has revealed it to us by his Spirit. It gives us the faith we need to push through each and every day. As believers, we see what others don't see, because we have the spirit of truth residing deep down in our soul. We have this spirit of truth inside of us, which gives us some of the same powers that Jesus had on earth.

#51: Nevertheless

Nevertheless, I tell you the truth. It is to your advantage that I go away; for if I do not go away, the Helper will not come to you; but if I depart, I will send Him to you.
—John 16:7

Sometimes, my parents used to say that I could not have any dessert with dinner until I ate my vegetables. I remember I would not finish all the vegetables, and, *nevertheless*, my parents would still give me the dessert. Merriam-Webster defines nevertheless as "however" or "in spite of." John 16:7 starts out with *"nevertheless,"* indicating that something is going to happen, although it probably should not happen. My parents gave me the dessert, although I didn't deserve it, since I didn't finish my vegetables. *Nevertheless,* they hoped that I would eat more vegetables later.

In the Bible, the disciples had been fishing all night, and they had caught nothing. They were on the shores of Galilee washing their nets. Washing their nets meant that they had given up, and saw that continuing to fish would not produce a catch. Jesus stopped by and noticed that the disciples were washing their nets. He encouraged them to continue fishing, although it was that time of day when men usually came in from fishing.

Luke 5:5 states, "Master," Simon replied, "we worked hard all last night and didn't catch a thing. But if you say so, I'll let the nets down again." And this time their nets were so full of fish they began to tear! Where it says, "But if you say so," some Bible translations say "nevertheless." The men had given up catching fish in their own strength, but Jesus encouraged them to try one more time. In spite of not catching any fish all night, the men were obedient to Jesus' command.

Jesus did so many miracles with the disciples that they did not want him to leave. But Jesus knew that He had to leave in order to save us from our sins. In John 16:7, He refers to the helper coming once He goes away. The helper, sometimes referred to as the comforter, is the Holy Spirit. He promised us that he would return one day, and until then, we have the comforter, the Holy Spirit. This comforter is the spirit of truth; it is the Christ-like power residing in our earthly bodies. Matthew 28:19-20 states, "Therefore go and make disciples of all nations, baptizing them in the name of the Father and of the Son and of the Holy Spirit, and teach them to obey everything I have commanded you. And surely I am with you always, to the very end of the age." This command is the great commission. Jesus told the disciples to baptize not just in His name and the Father, but he also told them to baptize in the Holy Spirit after His resurrection.

Jesus had to go away in order to give us this wonderful gift. The Holy Spirit will reside in us until Jesus returns for us. In order to receive this wonderful Holy Spirit, every man must bow to God and believe that Jesus died on the cross for our sins and that He rose on the third day. They must also confess their sins, and repent of wrongdoing. Although men and women today have a nature of sin, nevertheless, Christ died for our sins. We owe our lives to Him because of this great commission, and we must be forever thankful for the debt He paid for our lives. As a result, we have the comforter residing in our souls to give us hope for today and tomorrow.

#52: The Battle Is Not Ours

All those gathered here will know that it is not by sword or spear that the Lord saves;
for the battle is the Lord's, and he will give all of you into our hands.
—1 Samuel 17:47

Sometimes, we try to grab the bull by the horns and get the job done. We try to work out relationship problems without asking God to intervene in the situation. We try to handle our own financial struggles with our own strength. We try to get along with difficult people by reading self-help books. We become paralyzed by the actions of others, and we can't believe the way other people treat us. When we have done all that we can do, we continue to stand and trust God.

Jacob, who had lived a life of tricking his brother Esau and then later Laban, finally was challenged by God. Jacob wrestled all night with the Lord, but at the end, the Lord blessed him in a mighty way. Genesis 32:22-28 says, "That night Jacob got up and took his two wives, his two maidservants and his eleven sons and crossed the ford of the Jabbok. After he had sent them across the stream, he sent over all his possessions. So Jacob was left alone, and a man wrestled with him till daybreak. When the man saw that he could not overpower him, he touched the socket of Jacob's hip so that his hip was wrenched as he wrestled with the man. Then the man said, "Let me go, for it is daybreak." But Jacob replied, "I will not let you go unless you bless me." The man asked him, "What is your name?" "Jacob," he answered. Then the man said, "Your name will no longer be Jacob, but Israel, because you have struggled with God and with men and have overcome." Jacob had many struggles with his wife's father Laban, and he was blessed, as we read in the passage. One of his struggles before having his name changed to Israel was with God. This struggle was a spiritual battle, and it caused Jacob to limp the rest of his days. His name was changed forever because of his spiritual battle, and his name went down in history. In the same manner, when we are having a struggle, we just have to hold on like Jacob. Although Jacob's hip was knocked out of place, he held on to the man who may have been an angel of God.

The battles that we face are truly spiritual. Satan can enter his spirit into others, and it may seem that we are facing the devil himself. But we are facing an evil spirit that has entered the other person, and the best defense we have against the other person is to pray for him. We must also forgive that person if they hurt us or deceive us, because Jesus forgave us. Ephesians 6:12-13 states, "For our struggle is not against flesh and blood, but against the rulers, against the authorities, against the powers of this dark world, and against the spiritual forces of the evil in the heavenly realms." As this passage clearly states, our battle is truly not against flesh and blood, but we are facing the evil forces in the heavenly realm. The Holy Spirit must intervene and fight for us, because we can't fight with our physical strength. So often, we take the problem in our own hands without taking it to God in prayer, and asking God to work it out. Of course we need to wait patiently for God to intervene.

Romans 8:26-27 says, "In the same way, the Spirit helps us in our weaknesses. We do not know what we ought to pray for, but the Spirit himself intercedes for us with groans that words cannot express. And he who searches our hearts knows the mind of the Spirit, because the Spirit intercedes for the saints in accordance with God's will." The battle is truly not ours, but the Lord's to win for us.

#53: God's Power Is Sufficient

But he said to me, "My grace is sufficient for you, for my power is made perfect in weakness. Therefore I boast all the more gladly about my weaknesses, so that Christ power may rest on me. That is why, for Christ's sake, I delight in weaknesses, in insults, in hardships, in persecutions, in difficulties. For when I am weak, then I am strong."
—2 Corinthians 12:9-10

When we catch a cold or the flu, we drag along and realize that our bodies really need a boost from somewhere. We feel like we are on our last days. Sometimes, it takes sickness to realize that a Higher Power operates inside of us and makes everything work right. Many things work together so we can have movement, and we can use our body organs.

Think about the ball games where you put your best foot forward and the opposing team just keeps coming. You know that you're supposed to be winning, but the other team just keeps gaining ground. Or the times when you get in a financial crisis, and just don't know how it all is going to work out. These are the times when God works through our submission and humbleness.

In 2 Corinthians 12:9, God tells us that His grace is sufficient in our weakness. If we continue to achieve things in our own power, then we may become arrogant and not give God the praise and honor He deserves. In trials, it is actually better that we fail or come up short, because once we work through the situation and we don't know how we got through it, we know that God's power delivered us from our opponent or the evil one.

Oftentimes, a situation requires a miracle to continue on in a game or a life situation. It is the bottom of the ninth and two outs, and we need the worst hitter in the lineup to get a hit for us in order to win (or continue) the game. The ball doesn't always go the way that we want it, but when it does, we know that God has done the miraculous. No athlete or coach can take the credit, when they know that their strength didn't create the success. Sometimes, the faith has to be dwindled, and the light dimmed to a flicker before God shows up. But when He does, a comeback or a change for the good usually happens.

Remember the story of Sampson. Sampson did so many things with his own strength. He killed a lion with his own bare hands; he killed 1000 people with the jawbone of a donkey—he did so many miraculous things with his strength. He had to lose his strength before he relied on God's strength. Although he thought that his strength was coming from his long hair, his strength was actually coming from God.

People often get their strength from money, relationships, cars, fame, and large homes. All of these things are temporary, and eventually will decay over time. God must be first in all things. Sampson lost his hair, his sight, and probably lost some of his hope. But one last time he called on the name of the Lord, and God answered him in his weakest state. God's power was magnified in Sampson's weakness. Jesus Christ also humbled himself and became weak by dying on the cross for us. Through His submission and taking on our sins, this weak nature gave us the faith that we have and gave us eternal life. The power of Jesus raised Him on the third day, and the power took Him to the right hand of God. He left us with this same power, the Holy Spirit. We should thank Jesus for the Almighty power that is made strong in our weaknesses. We need to thank Him for the gift that He planted in our souls after we became His followers.

#54: Don't Let the Flame Go Out

For this reason, I remind you to fan into flame the gift of God, which is in
you through the laying on of my hands. For God did not give us a spirit
of timidity, but a spirit of power, of love, and of self-discipline.
—2 Timothy 1:6-7

Those individuals who do not read the Bible or know scripture often use the saying that they don't have a spirit of fear. In order to get a fire going, we need at least a spark or a flicker of fire. The verse before 2 Timothy 1:7 talks about fanning in the flame. If you have ever started a fire in an old farm house, you know what I mean. You need a little breeze or fan to get the fire going. By fanning the flicker or early flame, the fire takes full flame. Thus, the Holy Spirit works the same way. It starts with prayer, and the laying of hands by another Christian brother or sister. The power is transferred from one to the other. When we accept Jesus Christ in our life, the flame is transferred. This flame is the Holy Spirit. 1 Timothy 6, also states that this flame is a gift of God, which is something that we can't work for or earn through righteous living, but is given because we have faith in Jesus.

God has given us a confident spirit. He does not want us to fear anything, because feeling fear would mean we are not trusting in Him. God does tell us to have one fear, and that fear is God himself. Proverbs 1:7 states that the fear of the Lord is the beginning of wisdom. The only one that we need to fear is the one that can take the soul, and that is God. In Matthew 6:24, God clearly tells us not to be afraid of what we are going to eat, wear, and shelter. This confidence comes with the Holy Spirit that God gives to us for believing in Jesus Christ.

First, God gives us power through the Holy Spirit. In Philippians 4:13, God instructs us that we can do all things through Christ who strengthens us. As Christians, we have the same power that Jesus has, which allowed Him to rise from the dead. This power allows us to move mountains. This power allows us to encourage and heal others. God's power is sufficient for us, and it helps us mostly when we are weak, which allows glory to be given to God.

Second, when receiving Jesus as our Savior, one of the gifts of the Spirit is love. We are able to love like Jesus loved. In Mark 12:29-31, God gives us the greatest commandment: "The most important one," answered Jesus, "is this: 'Hear, O Israel, the Lord our God, the Lord is one. Love the Lord your God with all your heart, and with all your soul, and with your entire mind, and with all your strength. The second is this: Love your neighbor as yourself. There is no commandment greater than these." We first must love God with everything that we have, and second, we must love our neighbor. Jesus loved everyone, and we want to love our family, coworkers, teammates, and anyone that God puts in our path.

Third, God gives us self-discipline. We are able to gain some of the same discipline that Jesus had through the Holy Spirit in us. We gain discipline by praying, as Jesus went into the mountains to pray. We gain self-discipline by fasting and praying according to God's will for us to fast and pray, and we also gain discipline and accountability through fellowship with others.

#55: The Power Source

*But you will receive power when the Holy Spirit comes on you; and
you will be my witnesses in Jerusalem, and in all Judea, and
Samaria, and to the ends of the earth.*
—Acts 1:8

A modern-day lamp shines the brightest light, but it first must be connected to a power source by plugging it into an electrical outlet. In the same manner, a flashlight is able to give bright light as well, and its power source comes from batteries placed inside the device. A car is able to give flashing lights, and a car's power source starts with the battery. Our spiritual bodies operate in a similar fashion. To receive God's gift of the Holy Spirit, we need a power source. The power source begins when we connect with Jesus Christ, and accept him as our Savior. Through this belief, we are able to gain Christ-like power, which is the Holy Spirit.

Because we have the Holy Spirit, we now emit a bright light. We can know that others also have the Holy Spirit, because of the light that they are putting off, and also by their actions. Galatians 5:22-23 states, "But the fruit of the Spirit is love, joy, peace, patience, kindness, goodness, faithfulness, gentleness, and self-control. Against such things there is no law." If another Christian is operating in the spirit, then we should see all these qualities.

God wants us to be witnesses for Jesus Christ, as long as we believe in Jesus Christ. Now that we have the Spirit, we should enthusiastically share this great news with others. In Ephesians 3:14, God tells us what to do first before sharing the good news with others, and that first thing is to pray. The passage states, "I pray that out of His glorious riches He may strengthen you with power through His Spirit in your inner being." The inner being can be darkness or light. Once we accept Christ, then the inner being produces light. By witnessing to others, we are turning on the heart lights for Jesus. Athletes may refer to this inner being as drive or inner force. But it is something greater that God gives, which is hidden away in the heart—the Holy Spirit.

Matthew 28:19 gives us the great commission, stating, "Therefore go and make disciples of all nations baptizing them in the name of the Father and of the Son and of the Holy Spirit, and teaching them to obey everything I have commanded you. And surely I am with you always, to the very end of the age." Jesus gives us our job description in a few sentences in this passage, and we should obey because of His love for us and because He died for us. We should follow His instructions word for word. Jesus set the leadership pattern for all of us, and He tells us to continue the tradition and rise up more disciples to proclaim the great news. He also instructs us to baptize those who believe in the name of the Father, the Son, and the Holy Spirit.

Jesus also lets us know that obedience is also important, and we must instruct others to follow the commandments of God and be obedient to every word of God. We are encouraged in that God tells us that He is always with us, and that He is with us until the end of age. It is our duty to carry the word throughout our surroundings, and we must carry the word of God to every corner of the earth. 2 Corinthians 3:17 says, "Now the Lord is the Spirit, and where the Spirit of the Lord is, there is freedom." Once we have the Spirit, we are free from the chains of this world.

9

Jealousy

#56: The Spirit of Jealousy

As they danced, they sang: "Saul has slain his thousands, and David his tens of thousands." Saul was very angry; this refrain galled him. "They have credited David with tens of thousands," he thought, "but me with only thousands. What more can he get but the kingdom?" And from that time on, Saul kept a jealous eye on David. The next day, an evil spirit from God came forcefully upon Saul. He was prophesying in his house, while David was playing the harp, as he usually did. Saul had a spear in his hand and he hurled it, saying to himself, "I'll pin David to the wall." But David eluded him twice. Saul was afraid of David, because the Lord was with David but had left Saul.
—1 Samuel 18:7-11

Unfortunately, the spirit of jealousy has been around since the beginning of time. Satan became prideful, and wanted to be like God. Cain became jealous of his brother Abel, because God showed more interest in his offering. God is also a jealous God, but He is the almighty God. He is jealous when we put things in front of Him or when people make other earthly people or things their idol. We all have some form of jealousy, and it must be dealt with through prayer. We must ask God for contentment, and know that the circumstance that we are in is the state God would have us in.

Saul became jealous because the people were shouting that David had killed his 10 thousands, and Saul only his thousands. Saul, in his insecurity, started thinking that David may secure his kingdom someday, so Saul plotted to kill David. The Bible says that God sent an evil spirit upon Saul. Why would God send an evil spirit? Romans 8:28 tells us all things work for the good of God. Although a spirit of jealousy, an evil spirit, is a bad thing, it fulfilled God's purpose of getting David to become king. Sometimes, God has to let evil work for a little while, but then He always does what He says He is going to do. Nothing happens that God does not want to happen.

David was actually working for Saul, playing the harp for him. Saul tried to kill David with the spear, but David found a way to avoid it. David ran for his life, and sometimes that may be the best way to deal with a jealous person. It is better to move away from that person and pray. Saul tried to kill David again, and hurled a spear at him. David never struck back at Saul. He had a time for revenge, when he snuck in and cut a patch from Saul's clothing while he was sleeping. However, David showed Saul the patch, and let him know that he spared his life and wanted peace. David later became the King of Israel.

In dealing with jealousy, we may have to take the approach of David. David continued to honor Saul's authority and position, although he knew that Saul had a jealous spirit. He did avoid Saul, and did not give Saul an opportunity to kill him. Jealousy is a sure thing in this world. It happens in the marketplace, in the workplace, and in the church. We need to pray for these jealous people, and use wisdom as David did with Saul. When we see this tormenting spirit, we need to ask God to give us wisdom in how to deal with the situation. We learned in 1 John 4:4, "Greater is He that is in you than the one who is in the world." God has a Spirit of truth that far exceeds an evil or tormenting spirit. Psalm 37:4 says that God always gets the victory, and gives us the desires of our hearts. If God speaks to you through meditation and prayer, promising you a blessing, then let no one stand in the way of what God has already set forth.

#57: A Jealous Wife and a Jealous God

So she said to Abram, "The Lord has kept me from having children. Go, sleep with my maidservant; perhaps I can build a family through her." Abram agreed to what Sarai said. So after Abram had been living in Canaan ten years, Sarai, his wife, took her Egyptian maidservant, Hagar, and gave her to her husband to be his wife. He slept with Hagar, and she conceived. When she knew she was pregnant, she began to despise her mistress. Then Sarai said to Abram, "You are responsible for the wrong I am suffering."
—Genesis 16:2-5

One of the earlier acts of jealousy is found between Sarai and her maidservant. Both Abram and Sarai were advanced in age, and God had promised Abram that He would make his ancestors as numerous as the stars. Genesis 15:5 states, "He took him outside and said, "Look up at the heavens and count the stars—if indeed you can count them." Then he said to him, "So shall your offspring be." Like Abraham and Sarai, we become impatient, and act before God fulfills His promises to us that we have received from reading his word and through prayer. God had already spoken to Abram, promising him a generation as numerous as the stars. His wife Sarai was impatient, and she offered her maidservant to Abram so they could have a child, which was one of the first forms of adultery in the Bible. We knew that God is a jealous God—even before the Ten Commandments that were given to Moses. But we witness some major consequences from Abram sleeping with the maidservant, because the maidservant became envious of Sarai.

The maidservant's name was Hagar, and the Bible says that she despised Sarai once she became pregnant. But Sarai, who suggested that Abram took her maidservant and slept with her, then blamed Abram for the jealous maidservant. Because of the jealousy of the maidservant, Sarai threw her out of the house, and caused the son Ishmael to be raised without his father Abram. This situation caused a splitting of nations, because the covenant son Jacob was loved more by Abram and Sarai.

A similar act of jealousy happened with Peninnah and Hannah, who were the wives of Elkanah. Elkanah had two wives, and Peninnah was jealous of Hannah as he gave her more because he loved her more. 1 Samuel 1:5-6 states, "But to Hannah he gave a double portion because he loved her, and the Lord had closed her womb. And because the Lord had closed her womb, her rival kept provoking her in order to irritate her." It was an act of jealousy by Peninnah, but God would eventually give her a son, Samuel, through Elkanah.

These stories demonstrate that jealousy can lead to sin if not controlled. In Sarai's case, she stopped trusting God and, like Eve, she tempted the man to run ahead of God by sleeping with the maidservant Hagar, which caused hatred and jealousy. In Peninnah's case, she was jealous because Hannah received more from Elkanah. We need to think about where we can check our hearts, and ask God to remove any hatred.

#58: A Jealous Brother

Then the Lord said to Cain, "Why are you angry? Why is your face downcast?
If you do what is right, will you not be accepted? But if you do not do
what is right, sin is crouching at your door; it desires to have you, but you
must master it." Now Cain said to his brother Abel, "Let's go out to the field."
And while they were in the field, Cain attacked his brother Abel and killed him.
Then the Lord said to Cain, "Where is your brother Abel?"
"I don't know," he replied. "Am I my brother's keeper?"
—Genesis 4:6-9

The Bible story of Cain and Abel was one of the first forms of family jealousy. Abel gave his first and best produce to God, and God rewarded him with praise for doing so. Cain failed to give his first fruit from his portions, and God was not pleased with his offering. Cain became angry and perhaps jealous, because the Lord looked more favorable on his brother Abel's offering. God also warned Cain to be careful about his anger, and he warned him of the possibility of falling into deeper sin. Cain, with his jealous spirit, rose up and killed his own brother.

Just as we have jealousy in the family, we can also have jealousy in the extended family of teammates and coworkers. When people work together day in and day out, those individuals become somewhat of an extended family. Someone has to step up and make sure the family stays in unity. Especially in team dynamics, you cannot have every person leading the pack. The coach/leader has to see jealousy early on, and find ways for people to get along with each other. In families, the mother and father should pick up on envy, and quench those fires before they burn out of control. One question to ask is where were Adam and Eve? Why didn't they see this dual rivalry between the boys? Adam and Eve had fallen, and maybe because of that fall, they were not able to notice the hatred of Cain toward Abel. The brothers had a bigger parent to go to at that time, who was God himself. When God asked Cain about Abel, Cain answered, "Am I my brother's keeper?"

We are responsible for our actions, and yes, we are our brother's keeper. If we are on our face praying to the Lord, we are less likely to lash out at our brother. In the team dynamic of sports, the coach can ask God to remove the spirit of jealousy, and encourage teammates to love one another. In the workplace, when another coworker does better than we do, we need to recognize his efforts, and we need to pray that God will continue to bless him. The problem comes when one person thinks that he is losing ground. As a result, like Abel, he lashes out at his coworker or teammate. He doesn't go to the extreme that Cain did, but he hurts the person in other ways. Gossip is one way that a person can take away from his brother, and we do know that gossip is a sin. Ephesians 4:29 states, "Do not let any unwholesome talk come out of your mouths, but only what is helpful for building others up according to their needs, that it may benefit those who listen." Gossip has been compared to murder, because we are downgrading the reputation and character of the other person. Similar to Cain, we can also be hurting another person with the things that we are saying.

We need to check ourselves, and pray for those who envy us because we are doing the will of God. In the same manner, we need to check our hearts to see if hatred or jealousy exists that we need to deal with. We need to hold on to God's golden rule, and do unto others as we would want them to do to us. Build others up and serve one another.

#59: The Jealous King

Then Herod called the Magi secretly and found out from them the exact time the star had appeared. He sent them to Bethlehem and said, "Go and make a careful search for the child. As soon as you find him, report to me, so that I too may go and worship him."
—Matthew 2:7

We should be very happy when good things happen to other people, and the birth of Jesus was a special time of rejoicing. The wise men came and offered their gifts and praises. As had been promised, the Savior Jesus Christ was on earth in human form. The entire world should have been rejoicing because a new king was born, which was not the case with King Herod. He was jealous of the newborn king.

In today's world, some people greet us with a smile and act like they are interested in our achievements, while deep down inside, they are not happy about our success. How are these people able to hide their true feelings from us? Why don't we realize how they really feel about us? The answer is that sometimes it takes time to really see the heart of a person, and we have to wait for God to reveal the inner qualities of others. Over time, the jealous flaws in other characters wiggle their way out.

Herod acted as though he wanted to worship Jesus, but deep down inside he was plotting to find Jesus and kill the newborn king. God reveals how a person can praise us in one breath, but on the flipside, have menace in their hearts. In Matthew 2:13, God says, "When they had gone, an angel of the Lord appeared to Joseph in a dream. 'Get up,' he said, 'take the child and his mother and escape to Egypt. Stay there until I tell you, for Herod is going to search for the child to kill him.'" We have a just God and a fair God. We have a God that protects us from evil. Isaiah 54:17 states, "No weapon formed against you will prosper." When we are serving and giving God praise, He protects all who call upon His name.

God also showed favor to the wise men who came to worship Jesus. After giving praises and gifts to the newborn king, they were warned in a dream not to go back to the king. He was tricked by the Magi of the time and location of the birth of Jesus, so he ordered a death note on all the young sons of Israel, and, unfortunately, the jealousy of Herod resulted in the death of all the boys two years and under. Matthew 2:18 states, "A voice is heard in Ramah weeping and great mourning, Rachel weeping for her children and refusing to be comforted, because they are no more."

We saw similar jealous patterns in Judas Iscariot. Judas traveled alongside Jesus during His ministry time. Jesus already knew that Judas would deceive Him and backstab Him. We have to learn that not everyone on the team is for us or the team. In today's world, we sometimes have a Judas or a King Herod on our team, and through prayer and wise leadership, we need to ask God for protection from the enemy. Like God has revealed in His word, we have to endure these times because the weeds have to grow among the wheat. One day, the weeds are judged and thrown in the fire. We have to be the bigger person in these situations, pray for those who are trying to persecute us, and ask for God's healing and protecting hand. Just as when Jesus asked for God to take the cup off of Him, then followed that by saying that He wanted the Father's will to be done, the thing we need to do is pray for healing for those who come against us.

#60: Get Up Out of the Ashes

Then the Lord said to Satan, "Have you considered my servant Job? There is no one on earth like him; he is blameless and upright, a man who fears God and shuns evil. And he still maintains his integrity, though you incited me against him to ruin him without any reason." "Skin for skin!" Satan replied. "A man will give all he has for his own life. But stretch out your hand and strike his flesh and bones, and he will surely curse you to your face." The Lord said to Satan, "Very well, then, he is in your hands; but you must spare his life." So Satan went out from the presence of the Lord and afflicted Job with painful sores from the soles of his feet to the top of his head. Then Job took a piece of broken pottery and scraped himself with it as he sat among the ashes.
—Job 2:3-7

No one has more jealousy than the devil. He is the one who can operate through others, and he is the one who plants jealousy and envy in the hearts of others. When others are not following the will of God, Satan and his angels can move a demon into that person who will rise up against us. We have seen this situation throughout the Bible. We see how Cain, Judas, and others act out of their jealousy. Satan is always roaming the earth, looking for someone to devour. The great thing is that we have God's protection, and Satan can do no more than God allows him to do. Satan is jealous of all Christians, because long ago he was cast out of God's presence and he has no hope. He is jealous of us, because he can never have what we have. We have a promised and sure victory from the sting of death, whereas Satan will never taste this victory. With this knowledge, we know the devil will do anything in his power to set traps and deceive us. Luke 22:31-32 states, "Simon, Simon, Satan has asked to sift you as wheat. But I have prayed for you, Simon, that your faith may not fail. And when you have turned back, strengthen your brothers." Like testing Job, Satan wanted to tempt and test the disciples in the same way.

Job was attacked by the devil, similar to what Jesus later faced. Job lost everything because of the jealousy of the devil. The whole thing was a test. When we are attacked similar to Job we just have to hold on to our faith, which is what Job did, and during his time of trouble, his own wife asked him to curse God and die. But Job was a righteous man, and God had given Satan permission to attack him and do as he pleased except taking his life. This example gives us encouragement, because no matter what we are going through, we know that God will not let the devil or others do anything without His permission. And because we know that God is on our side, we know that we will come through victorious no matter what trial we are facing.

As Job sat among the ashes, he was depressed after losing his family and his material possessions, and then he was faced with an illness of infections on his skin. Satan thought that he had won. But God redeemed Job and gave him what he needed to endure the test of the devil. Like Job, we have to hold on to our faith when the hard times come. We have to press forward, although the walls of life are pressing in on us. Nothing is too big for God, and He has told us in John 16:33 that we are going to have trouble in this world, but His Son Jesus has overcome this world. We have the Holy Spirit in us, which allows us to endure life's most difficult times. The Holy Spirit intercedes for us during these times and helps us during prayer and while fighting the battles in the spiritual realm. We need to hold on to God's healing hand, and not give the devil anything to rejoice.

#61: After All

Many among the crowds at the Temple believed in him (Jesus). "After all," they said, "would you expect the Messiah to do more miraculous signs than this man has done?" When the Pharisees heard that the crowds were whispering such things, they and the leading priests sent temple guards to arrest Jesus. But Jesus told them, "I will be with you only a little longer. Then I will return to the one who sent me. You will search for me but not find me. And you cannot go where I am going." The Jewish leaders were puzzled by this statement. "Where is he planning to go?" they asked. "Is he thinking of leaving the country and going to the Jews in other lands? Maybe he will even teach the Greeks! What does he mean when he says, "You cannot go where I am going?"
—John 7:31-34

All of us have a choice to make, and the choice is to choose life or death. Many people don't believe in God, and many don't believe Jesus was the Son of God and the Messiah who saved us from our sins. Even thousands of years ago, people doubted whether Jesus was the real deal. He performed many miracles, and some of the people believed. But we know today that we don't have to do things in order to be Christians, but we have healing power because of our faith in Jesus and because He died for our sins. He rose on the third day, and He brought victory to all of us. Many people doubt that Jesus is the Savior, and they cast envy upon those who do believe in Jesus. In John 7:31, the Bible uses the statement "after all," meaning that after all that Jesus had done, enough signs existed showing that Jesus is the Son of God. What is our "after all"?

After all, I believe in Jesus because I have seen the many miracles that He has brought me through. I have watched countless times how Jesus has delivered me from chronic illnesses. I have watched how God has answered prayers that didn't seem to manifest. I have watched how God has operated through others, and met their prayers and needs. I have, countless times, watched God silence the devil, and I know that God can protect us from the arrows of the enemy. "After all," Jesus did rise on the third day, and He has gone and prepared a place for us. The Jewish leaders didn't understand what Jesus meant when he said, "You cannot go where I am going." God hides his truths from the world, and the meaning of life is hidden in His word. Jesus told us that He had to go away, but He would come back, and He also let us know that He had prepared a place for us all. In John 14:3 Jesus says, "…and if I go and prepare a place for you, I will come back and take you to be with me that you also may be where I am. You know the way to the place where I am going." This passage gives us comfort, because we know through our beliefs and through the grace of God, we will one day be joined with the Lord.

Most of the world is envious of believers, because their hearts are hard to the truth of the word of God. They fail to understand or believe that Jesus is the only way to salvation, and Jesus is the way to eternal life. Many people store up for this short season on earth, and fail to realize that it is the short part of the journey. We have to prepare for our destination, and that is to be in heaven with Jesus. In John 14:6, Jesus answered, "I am the way and the truth and the life." "After all," Jesus did rise on the third day. Many are envious of Jesus Christ, because they don't want to believe that He is the way to the truth.

#62: Another Jealous Brother

Esau held a grudge against Jacob because of the blessing his father had given him. He said to himself, "The days of mourning for my father are near; then I will kill my brother Jacob. " When Rebekah was told what her older son Esau had said, she sent for her younger son Jacob and said to him, "Your brother Esau is consoling himself with the thought of killing you. Now then, my son, do what I say: Flee at once to my brother Alban in Haran. Stay with him for a while until your brother's fury subsides. When your brother is no longer angry with you and forgets what you did to him, I'll send word for you to come back from there. Why should I lose both of you in one day?"
—Genesis 27:41-45

Jealousy is heavy among the family, and sometimes jealousy can be in both parties. All along, Jacob had been thinking about the blessing of his older brother. In a way, the envy started first with the younger son. In Bible times, the older son received the initial blessing from the father. Also, the mother Rebekah loved Jacob more than she loved Esau. Esau was favored by the father, because he was a hunter and provided the best of meals for his father. Jealousy caused the family to be divided.

In the same manner, in our athletic circles and in the office place, we get jealous if the coach of the organization casts favoritism upon certain athletes. Sometimes, coaches and bosses feel an obligation to play the senior players in college because they are almost done. Sometimes, bosses feel an obligation to promote the older folk, because of time on the job, but not whether the person is good for the job. As we read of the interaction of Jacob and Esau, we see two brothers who are fighting for their father's throne.

Jacob used more wisdom than Esau. Esau came in hungry one day, and he asked Jacob for a meal. Jacob said he would give him the meal only if Esau agreed to give up his birthright. Esau lacked wisdom, and he basically sold his father's blessings for a hot meal, which was a major mistake. He envied his brother, because Jacob and Rebekah tricked Isaac by having Jacob dress up as Esau. One day Isaac asked Esau to go hunt him some game and bring it back. He blessed Esau first, since he was the first born son. While Esau was out hunting, Rebekah instructed Jacob to dress up as Esau and cook his father Isaac a hot meal. He took the meal into his father, and he also covered his skin with fur to appear to be hairy like Esau. Esau was furious and envious of his brother, because Isaac, being blind at the time, thought it really was Esau. Jacob moved away for 20 years to his mother's relatives, where he lived with Laban's family. The jealous brothers eventually had peace with each other.

This story is a case where jealousy existed in the family, and both parents showed favoritism, which caused problems. Perhaps, both parents should have spent equal time with both Jacob and Esau, but the situation resulted in Jacob leaving home because Esau had threatened his life. Jealousy can be a deadly sin. Proverbs 14:30 says, "A sound heart is the life of the flesh, but envy is the rottenness of the bones." The Bible also states in James 3:14, "But if ye have bitter envying and strife in your hearts, glory not, and lie not against the truth."

Jealousy over material possessions resulted in two brothers being mad at each other for many years. We need to think about what envy and jealousy we are carrying today against a teammate, a coach, a family member, or a teacher. We need to get it right with God.

10

Forgiveness

#63: Because He Forgave, We Too Must Forgive

Jesus said, "Father, forgive them, for they do not know what they are doing." And they divided up his clothes by casting lots.
—Luke 23:34

What would you do in your final hour if people were rejoicing over your death? If you could get back at them, would you lash out? When people come against us, the natural tendency is to lash back at them. It is human nature to fight back at others who persecute or take advantage of us. Some people wait until the appropriate time, and pay evil for evil. This behavior is not the trait of the Son of God, Jesus Christ. He had the power to fight back, but for our sake, He remains humble and died on the cross for us. Jesus forgave us of our sins, and God forgave us of our sins by giving Jesus to us. Because God gave Jesus to us as a perfect sacrifice, we should obey the commandments of God and live our lives with scripture. Jesus went through the most painful and humiliating death that anyone could face and He looked at all of his persecutors eye-to-eye as He went through the suffering that they inflicted upon him. In Luke 23:34, His answer was, "Father, forgive them, for they do not know what they are doing."

We have also done some persecuting in our time. Jesus had nothing to ask God for, because He was a perfect sacrifice. His forgiveness was to ask God for our forgiveness. Unlike Jesus, some things happen that we have to look back on in life, including people that we may have let down or sinned against. It is important that we do what Jesus did, and ask God to forgive us for our shortcomings. One of the familiar scriptures is found in John 3:16, which states, "For God so loved the world that He gave His one and only Son, that whoever believes in him shall not perish but have eternal life." For God did not send His Son into the world to condemn the world, but to save the world through Him. We can't have eternal life through our good works and acts of pure morality. We must believe that Jesus is the Son of God, and ask God to forgive us of our sins, and turn away from our sins. We must believe that Jesus died on the cross for our sins, and He got up on the third day defeating the sting of death.

After asking God to forgive us of our sins, we must do what Jesus did on the cross. We must forgive those who have come against us and sinned against us. Others exist who did everything but hang us on the cross. We have had people tell lies about us, and we have had others slander our names through gossip. We have had relationships that fell on the rocks, and we have faced and gone through challenging marriages. Some of us have had a loved one walk away. We have had people steal money from us, and people who borrow but fail to pay the money back. Like Jesus Christ, we have also been persecuted by others, and in order to follow the will of God, we have to forgive others, no matter how severe the hurt or infliction of wrongdoing.

Jesus said it all on the cross when he said, "For they do not know what they are doing." We have to understand that the people who come against us don't realize that they are hurting us, and they don't feel or bear our pain. Jesus felt all of our past, present, and future pains, and He took all of it to the cross. We hurt too, because as Christians, we are persecuted and we bear many of the same pains as Jesus did. Those sinning against us do not know what they are doing because they are either lost or their hearts are not yet right with God. They may be in a dry season, allowing the enemy to use them in a bad way.

#64: The Rolling Stones

The teachers of the law and the Pharisees brought in a woman caught in adultery. They made her stand before the group and said to Jesus, "Teacher, this woman was caught in the act of adultery. In the law, Moses commanded us to stone such women. Now what do you say?" They were using this question as a trap, in order to have a basis for accusing Him. But Jesus bent down and started to write on the ground with his finger. When they kept on questioning Him, he straightened up and said to them, "If any one of you is without sin, let him be the first to throw a stone at her." Again, he stooped down and wrote on the ground. At this, those who heard began to go away one at a time, the older ones first, until only Jesus was left, with the woman still standing there. Jesus straightened up and asked her, "Woman, where are they? Has no one condemned you?" "No one, sir," she said. "Then neither do I condemn you," Jesus declared. "Go now and leave your life of sin."
—John 8:3-11

This scripture is devotion in itself, and if we said nothing at all we would have the message. The teachers of the law were trying to trick Jesus, and so they wanted to see if Jesus would forgive the woman. Although by law, Moses would have had the woman stoned to death. Jesus nonchalantly stirred the ground with his finger, and He did not look at their sin. They were looking at the speck in the woman's eyes, but failed to realize the log in their own eyes. Perhaps Jesus was praying for the woman and the people as He was writing in the sand. I think that Jesus wrote in the sand to give them time to think about what they were doing. Some of them still were not getting it, so He straightened up, and said that any of them without sin could cast the first stone. All of the teachers of the law and others walked away sad that day, because they realized their sins as well.

Jesus went back to writing in the sand, perhaps praying for the woman to get right with God. Then, He got up a second time and asked the woman where all the people went. But Jesus is the Son of God, and He knew that no one was left, just as when God was about to destroy Sodom and Gomorrah, and Abraham kept asking God to spare the city if anyone there was righteous. By the time Abraham got down to less than 10 people, he realized that no one in Sodom was right with God. But God spared the city long enough to get his nephew Lot out. When Jesus straightened up the second time, he told the woman that He did not condemn her either for her sin, and He specifically told her to go and sin no more.

We need to take the log out of our eye, and stop looking at the speck in our brother's eye. My sister once told me, "You have to sweep around your own doorstep," which means that before we say our neighbor has a dirty yard or has sin in his life, we have to get our own life right with God. We have to drop our stones like the teachers of the law did many years ago. A lot of stones were dropped that day, and many were rolling around on the ground. As the saying goes, "a rolling stone gathers no moss." If we ever pick up a stone to condemn, we should quickly drop it. We need to remember that Jesus is the cornerstone, and as long as we repent of our sins and believe in Jesus, we too can walk away from a life of sin and have salvation. After the cross, Jesus rolled away the biggest stone.

#65: Caught in the Net

Jesus said, "If you forgive men when they sin against you,
your heavenly Father will also forgive you."
—Matthew 6:14

Fishing is a great sport in itself, and it allows us a pastime. If a person is fishing for a trade, then using a large net would yield more fish in less time. I remember an old saying, "If you give a man a fish, you feed him for a day. If you teach a man how to fish, then you feed him for life."

The enemy has nets as well, and he is trying to trap us in his nets. If people know of danger or know that trouble is coming, they of course dodge it. No one spreads a net in front of his prey, or else they would go around it. Proverbs 1:17 states, "How useless to spread a net in full view of all the birds!" In the same manner, Satan does not show himself in the physical realm nor does he reveal himself in the daylight. Even fish are able to dodge a baited hook in the water. The devil uses one of the craftiest ways to trap us, and take us out of the will of God. He uses unforgivingness.

Are we a catch of the enemy? We first have to forgive ourselves. Jesus died for our sins for the past, present, and future. 1 Peter 3:18 says, "For Christ died for sins once for all, the righteous for the unrighteous, to bring you to God." We have assurance that Jesus Christ's blood covered all our sins, and that does not give us the right to keep on sinning. A change of heart should occur. 2 Corinthians 5:17 states, "Therefore, if anyone is in Christ, he is a new creation; the old has gone, the new has come!" Thus, we must push forward for what Jesus Christ has stored up for us. We need to know that we are free from any trap, and the devil will not discourage us. We must put on a new attitude, which comes from the Holy Spirit, and we must push forward in the name of Jesus.

The biggest snare of the enemy is getting people to be unforgiving toward other people. Most of the time, unforgiving people hurt forgiving people. In other words, people who are hurting, hurt other people, and those who cannot forgive in their hearts tend to cause those who are forgiving to fall into this same pattern. It is the work of the enemy. It is the trap that the devil has set. As stated in Ephesians 6:12, which was discussed earlier, "We are not fighting against flesh and blood, but we fight against the evil forces in the heavenly realm."

How does this situation happen? Someone does something to us, or we go through a divorce or breakup. We also may have someone who steals something from us, or they gossip about us. Whatever it is, we must forgive them, because Jesus forgave our shortfalls. No matter how bad someone wronged us, we have to forgive them. Jesus suffered on the cross more than any of us can imagine, and He still asked God to forgive us.

#66: Forgive Before the Dream

Then Joseph could no longer control himself before all his attendants, and he cried out, "Have everyone leave my presence!" So there was no one with Joseph when he made himself known to his brothers. And he wept so loudly that the Egyptians heard him, and Pharaohs' household heard about it. Joseph said to his brothers, "I am Joseph! Is my father still living?" But his brothers were not able to answer him, because they were terrified at his presence. Then Joseph said to his brothers, "Come close to me." When they had done so, he said, "I am your brother Joseph, the one you sold into Egypt! And now, do not be distressed and do not be angry with yourselves for selling me here, because it was to save lives that God sent me ahead of you."
—Genesis 45:1-5

We have all taken the wrong turn on the highway, and ended up seeing something wonderful or meeting someone new. I remember one of my journeys to Hampton Roads, when I got lost in the Williamsburg area. I was running late for an appointment, and because of the backed-up traffic, I decided to try the back roads. I ended up in Yorktown, VA, along a waterside, and it was extremely breathtaking and beautiful. All of the years that I lived in the area, I had never visited Yorktown. I promised myself that I would go back one day. It definitely was a road less traveled.

We all have detours in life. In Genesis, we read where Joseph's life had a major detour. After telling his brothers his dreams, they became jealous and threw him into a pit and sold him into slavery. Joseph was falsely accused by Potiphar's wife and ended up in prison. How could he forever forgive his brothers who threw him in the pit? How could he forever forgive Potiphar's wife, who falsely accused him of trying to make a pass at her? In time, God has a way of mending our hearts. Although he served time in prison, Joseph continued to pass his dream on to others. He must have spent many nights crying himself to sleep from his brothers hurting him, and he also probably had a lot of self-pity.

But God picked him up. Joseph became the best dreamer in the city and saved the land from famine. The dreams were of seven fat cows and seven skinny cows. Joseph was able to foresee seven years of good times, and he saw seven good years. The king Pharaoh put Joseph over all of the affairs of his estate. Joseph's dream came true. His brothers came to Egypt, and they had to bow to Joseph. He could have punished his brothers as they punished him, but he wept and asked them to come closer.

In the same manner, when God pulls us through a difficult time, we must pray for those who have come against us, and remember all who have hurt us. Joseph had long forgiven his brothers, because if not, he would not have asked them to come closer. He moved his whole family to the land of Egypt, and his father was proud of him.

Joseph teaches us that no matter how bad we are hurt by others, even our family members, we have to go on. We have to pick up the pieces, and continue helping others. One day, like Joseph, we will be helping the King himself. In reality, we are already helping the main king, and that King is Jesus Christ. For everything that we do for others brings glory to God. We need to help others achieve their dreams.

#67: Turn the Other Cheek

Peter came to Him and asked, "Lord, how often should
I forgive someone who sins against me? Seven times?"
"No!" Jesus replied, "seventy times seven!"
—Matthew 18:21-22

In a boxing match, a champion has to be prepared to get hit. If the champion boxer plays it safe the entire time, then he will not be able to advance. In order to score points, the champion boxer must engage the enemy. Oftentimes, the enemy does not fight fair, and possibly uses schemes and tactics that break the rules. I remember after Mike Tyson bit Evander Holyfield on the ear, Holyfield still continued with the fight. Tyson bit him a second time, and of course he was disqualified. After the fight, Holyfield still respected him. A champion requires good sportsmanship, and Holyfield still had respect for his opponent even after Tyson did him wrong. He still forgave him for his wrong actions.

Jesus took blow after blow before He bore the cross for us. In similar fashion to a modern day heavyweight fight, He forgave those who persecuted Him. He was flogged to the point of death, and then He was forced to carry His cross. He was nailed to the cross, and He was pierced in his side. He took all that punishment, and He still asked God to forgive the people for what they were doing. What would we have done? We may have tried to struggle and fight back, but Jesus Christ modeled the type of behavior that He would want us to have. We still need to forgive those who hurt us, no matter how painful the situation might be. Peter denied Jesus three times right in the heat of His arrest, and Jesus still forgave him for fleeing. Jesus taught us that we forgive indefinitely. In Matthew 18:21-22, He told us to forgive a person who sins against us seventy times seven.

Sometimes, it is better to just turn the other cheek. In Matthew 5:39, Jesus definitely turned the other cheek during his death on the cross. Although He had the power to come down, and strike back at those who were persecuting Him, He died for all humanity. He was the bigger one in the situation, and this model is the pattern we must have. When we are wronged by others, we must turn the other cheek, which is easier said than done. How do we move on from broken relationship? How do we move on when we get wrongly fired from a job? The main thing to remember is that when we hold something against others for hurting us, we can't move forward and it causes us to sin. We have to forgive the person, and move on.

Proverbs 25:21 says that if our enemy is hungry, we should feed him—again, easier said than done. God wants us to pay evil for good. We need to let God be the one who brings the guilt and persecution on that person. We are not to do anything in our strength. If we help those who are persecuting us, they will stop and realize that they are the ones with the problem. We do not have to give in to their shortfalls and sins, but we need to continue to follow God's will and serve those people as long as the situation lines up with God's word. The best thing that we can do is pray for them, and God will give us the strength to work with them. We can't hate them if we are praying for their healing, and if we are praying and asking God to forgive them. It works every time when we ask God to forgive them.

#68: Satan's Trap

It is not an enemy who taunts me—I could bear that. It is not my foes
who so arrogantly insult me—I could have hidden from them. Instead, it
is you, my equal, my companion and close friend. What good fellowship
we once enjoyed as we walked together to the house of God.
—Psalm 55:12-14

It is a vicious cycle: first, we love and trust, then we get hurt, then we hurt, and then we hate. This sequence starts in the first grade, and it may happen throughout our lifetime. It goes from trust to love, then to hurt and hate. It is a trap of the enemy. In John Bevere's book, *The Bait of Satan,* he talks about how the enemy uses those closest to us to hurt us, and then we hate that person after they hurt us. How do we get past those who hurt us? We have to look toward Jesus, the author and finisher of our faith. Satan uses the bait of someone hurting us, and this hurt causes us to hate the other person. We learned earlier that if we hate someone else then we can't enter God's presence. We have to forgive the individual or individuals who hurt us. Many times, those who are closest to us, such as family members, hurt us the most. We have to find a way to forgive them.

Love is a wonderful thing to have for another person. Once we start loving, then we are vulnerable to being hurt. Psalm 55:12 says, "It is not an enemy who taunts me." In other words, if it was a stranger who caused the hurt, then it would not be as painful. In the same verse, David, the author of Psalms, says that if his enemies had hurt him, he could have hidden from them.

King David had to flee from King Saul, who heavily pursued him to hurt him. King David's statement that those who walked together with us to the house of God let us know that other Christians can hurt us as well. We get hurt, and we automatically lose faith in that person, and some people lose faith in God. It could be a job loss, a divorce, a financial loss, and/or a broken relationship. The person who we loved caused us to doubt and become disheartened.

If we are not careful, then hate quickly moves in for that person. This is the bait of Satan. If we hate another person, we are out of the will of God. We must first forgive ourselves, and then forgive the other person. If we look deep enough, we may have had something to do with the situation. We may have hurt that person earlier in the relationship, but when we are going through the pain we can only see their faults. We have to remember that the devil operates through others. The devil deceived Eve in the garden, and the devil entered into Judas. If the devil can enter into them, then he can enter into our loved ones and into us if we are not right with God. If we do things that are not in the will of God, we can be the one causing the hurt. We are then helping the enemy put the bait on the hook, because we now have others hating us. This situation causes another person to stumble. We need to think about who have we hurt who will no longer talk to us and who we need to call to rectify things. This forgiveness thing works two ways. We have hurt others, and we have also been hurt by others.

We know how Satan tries to trip us up. He wants us to hate one another. We need to get it right with this prayer: Lord, I pray and forgive those who have come against me. And Lord, I ask that you forgive me for those I have hurt and forgive me for the people who I hurt that I was not aware of. I ask this prayer in Jesus' name, amen.

#69: Blinded by the Light

Meanwhile, Saul was uttering threats with every breath and was eager to kill the Lord's followers. So he went to the high priest. He requested letters addressed to the synagogues in Damascus, asking for their cooperation in the arrest of any followers of the Way he found there. He wanted to bring them—both men and women—back to Jerusalem in chains. As he was approaching Damascus on this mission, a light from heaven suddenly shone down around him. He fell to the ground and heard a voice saying to him, "Saul! Saul! Why are you persecuting me?"
—Acts 9:1-3

Some of us have been down that same road that Saul was on. But then we are knocked flat on our face by life, and we really see the Lord for the first time. In 2001, I went to the hospital with an irregular heartbeat. That night, a man died beside me, and I started thinking that man could have been me. The following year, one morning after a football game, I woke up with all my joints swollen, as well as swollen lymph nodes. I could barely breathe. I thought the worst, and just knew it was cancer. I remember crying my eyes out at the Eastern Virginia Medical School, and I promised God that day if He would heal me from whatever was crippling me, I would give the rest of my life to Him. My cancer test and my HIV test came up negative. I have kept my promise, although like everyone else I have not been perfect. I was diagnosed with rheumatoid arthritis, which is a crippling disease. It was very humiliating, especially since I was a successful bodybuilder and strength coach. It took a while to start walking normally again, but God did answer my prayer and I can still work today with the disease. This experience changed my life forever. I try to stay committed to the word daily.

Saul was actually persecuting Christians and not living for the Lord. One day he was hit by a very bright light. In Acts 9:2, God yelled out to him saying, "Saul! Saul! Why are you persecuting me?" Jesus spoke directly to Saul, and let him know that it was He whom Saul was persecuting. When we hurt others or do not live according to God's word, it is not others who we are persecuting, but it is Jesus Himself who we are persecuting. Saul was blinded by the light that got his attention. Some people led him into the city, because he was blind. A believer named Ananias was asked by God to lay His hands on Saul, which would change Saul's life forever. In Acts 9:15-16, God instructed Ananias in this way: But the Lord said, "Go, for Saul is my chosen instrument to take my message to the Gentiles and to Kings, as well as to the people of Israel. And I will show him how much he must suffer for my name's sake." Saul was healed. Then Acts 9:18-19 says, "Instantly something like scales fell from Saul's eyes, and he regained his sight. Then he got up and was baptized. Afterward, he ate some food and regained his strength."

How does this situation relate to forgiveness? God forgave Saul for his sins, and the Bible says that he used to persecute Christians. God also saved a wretch like me, who used anabolic steroids at age 21 and also used to be fond of the ladies and drinking. I have seen the work that God has done in my life. We should not wait until God trips us up with life before we come in. All we have to do is ask Him for forgiveness. He washes us clean, and He forgives our sins from the east to the west. If God can forgive us, then we can forgive ourselves. We need to confess and ask for forgiveness.

11

Relationships

#70: A Leader's Home

The saying is sure: whoever aspires to the office of bishop desires a noble task. Now a bishop must be above reproach, married only once, temperate, sensible, respectable, hospitable, an apt teacher, not a drunkard, not violent but gentle, not quarrelsome, and not a lover of money. He must manage his own household well, keeping his children submissive and respectful in every way—for if someone does not know how to manage his own household, how can he take care of God's church?

—1 Timothy 3:1-5

Being in a leadership position is a noble task. Luke 12:48 says, "But the one who did not know and did what deserved a beating will receive a light beating. From everyone to whom much has been given, much will be required; and from the one to whom much has been entrusted, even more will be demanded." Many tasks come with a leadership position, and the leader must lead by example without embarrassment.

A leader should do everything in his power to reserve his marriage. The Bible says that a leader should marry only once. God does allow some exceptions to being married more than once, and that is if one person commits adultery. God gives us exact instructions on dealing with divorce. Matthew 5:31-33 reads, "It has been said, 'Anyone who divorces his wife must give her a certificate of divorce.' But I tell you that anyone who divorces his wife, except for marital unfaithfulness, causes her to become an adulterous, and anyone who marries the divorced woman commits adultery. Again, you have heard that it was said to the people long ago, do not break your oath, but keep the oaths you have made to the Lord." When we make a promise to God, we must keep it to the best of our ability. If the other person walks away from the marriage, then we want to attempt to reconcile the marriage. Adultery is the only grounds for separation and divorce, and even then, we must ask God to forgive if that happens with either party.

Several other qualities are expected as a leader, which are temperate, sensible, hospitable, an apt teach, not a drunkard, gentle and not quarrelsome, and not a lover of money. All of these qualities summed up spell leadership. A leader must be friendly in the home and at work. A leader must be a great teacher. A leader in any capacity must stay away from alcohol. A leader must offer his heart before asking for a hand. A leader must be careful about loving money. The Bible speaks directly on this last quality. 1 Timothy 6:10 says, "For the love of money is a root of all kinds of evil. Some people, eager for money, have wandered from the faith and pierced themselves with many griefs." It is the love of money that we must control. Money itself is not inherently evil because it can be used to give gifts and bless the kingdom.

Last, the Bible says that a leader should manage his household well, and if his home life is not managed well, then it possibly will eventually start revealing itself at work. The Bible speaks clearly on how to raise children. Proverbs 22:6 says, "Train children in the right way, and when they are old, they will not stray." Leadership expert John Maxwellhas said, "My definition of success [is] that those who know you the best love and respect you the most. There's something wrong with us when those who know us the least like us the best." We must put God first in our life, family second, and athletics should always come in third.

#71: Exchange Hate for Love

Blessed are you when people hate you, and when they exclude
you, revile you, and defame you on account of the Son of Man.
Rejoice in that day and leap for joy, for surely your reward is great
in heaven; for that is what their ancestors did to the prophets.
—Luke 6:22-23

No matter where you coach or lead, difficult people will be on your team. Difficult people are hard to relate to personally, and usually conflict and indecisive motives exist when relating to them. Often, it is a personality conflict. Matthew 10:22-23 states, "And you will be hated by all because of my name. But the one who endures to the end will be saved. When you are persecuted in one place, flee to another." This scripture is telling us to change our situation every time distress occurs, but you have to remember that if the world persecuted Jesus then they will surely persecute you because of what you believe. The best thing you can do in this situation is drown the difficult person with kindness. You have to turn the other cheek as God tells us to do. Eventually, that person will become a supporter of what you are trying to accomplish. You don't have to hang out with this person, but it would be advantageous that you show kindness and love to him, and he will see God in you. When you get into a heated confrontation with this person, you are not doing God's will, and it's best to flee as the scripture states. It's better to cool off than to act in anger. Proverbs 6:19 tells us that one of the things that God hates is a man who causes conflict with brothers.

#72: Your Spouse Has to Be Your Best Friend

*Each of you, however, should love his wife as himself,
and a wife should respect her husband.*
—Ephesians 5:33

Editor's Note: This lesson is written specifically for coaches, but the overall message applies to both coaches and athletes.

In sports today, a winning record alone does not guarantee a re-signing of a contract or the continuation of working standards. God tells us in Colossians 3:23, "Whatever your task, put yourselves into it, as done for the Lord and not for your masters." It is the Lord Christ you are serving; anyone who does wrong will be repaid for his wrong, and no favoritism exists. Many coaches pull 16- to 18-hour days, and wonder why their spouses are leaving them. Proverbs 16:25 says, "There is a way that seems right to a man, but in the end it leads to death." Nothing should come before God, and second, nothing should come before your spouse and children except God.

We all need to work, but a man is lost without his family, and he will not realize that until it's too late. If the ship is wrecked at home, then it will influence a leader's performance at work. No escape exists for that situation, and alcohol and adultery can only stain it for a little while. As stated in Luke 9:23-27, "Then he said to them all, 'If any want to become my followers, let them deny themselves and take up their cross daily and follow me. For those who want to save their life will lose it, and those who lose their life for my sake will save it. What does it profit them if they gain the whole world, but lose or forfeit themselves? Those who are ashamed of me and of my words, of them the Son of Man will be ashamed when He comes in his glory and the glory of the Father and of the holy angels. But I tell you, there are some standing here who will not taste death before they see the kingdom of God."

Those 18-hour days in the office mean that your children and spouse are missing valuable time with you, and with better allocation and delegation of your coaching/leadership duties, you should be home to spend time with them. We all have read of the many coaches who spent the night in their office, trying to figure out schemes to defeat opponents. As the scripture says, we must deny ourselves and remember what is important. What's more important? Winning a championship or raising your own child? Many coaches will say, my wife will never leave me or cheat on me, but Satan is busy. If we are not there, we are leaving the door open for the enemy to intrude our homes and relationships. God says in Proverbs 18:22, "He who finds a wife finds a good thing, and obtains favor from the Lord." Who would want to lose favor from the Lord? We must love and respect our spouses, because they are a gift from God. Take care of your home first, and then everything else will fall in place at work. Another verse in Proverbs 12:4 says, "A good wife is the crown of her husband, but she who brings shame is like rottenness in his bones." Proverbs 19:13 states, "A stupid child is ruin to a father, and a wife's quarreling is a continual dripping of rain." We must please our spouses in all ways, and make it a point to serve them. If not, they will not be happy.

Finally, keep your priorities in order using the three F's rule: God first, family second, and the field of play third. If you are an athlete, then apply the four F's rule: God first, family second, finals and tests third, and the field of play last. Many athletes put athletics first, academics second, and God third or fourth.

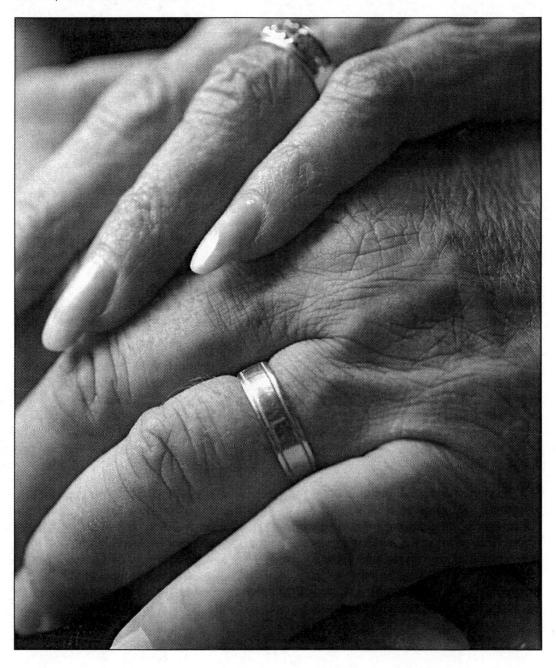

#73: Service + Love + Respect = Relationship

*After He had washed their feet, had put on His robe, and had
returned to the table, He said to them, "Do you know what I have
done to you? You call me Teacher and Lord—and you are right, for
that is who I am. So if I, your Lord and Teacher, have washed your
feet, you also ought to wash one another's feet. For I have set you
an example, that you also should do as I have done to you. Very
truly, I tell you, servants are not greater than their master, nor are
messengers greater than the one who sent them."*
—John 13:12-16

Editor's Note: This lesson is written specifically for coaches, but the overall message applies to
both coaches and athletes.

The first step in developing relationships is to let your team know that they are important to
you. As the leader, you can demonstrate this act of importance by continuing to support your
associates and look for ways to improve their personal and professional development. Another
way to demonstrate that you care is to see each of your associates as an important part of the
team. This same principle should hold true in the family or working environment. One child
should not receive favor over another child. The leader has to demonstrate love and service
first, which is an act of respect, and then the associates will also get on board and demonstrate
respect in return. It starts with the leader. The leader always has to be first in the battle. When
associates are not doing a job well, then perhaps the leader has not put all her heart into training
them.

Jesus made sure that He showed us the leadership pattern to follow. In order to wash their
feet, He had to have a great relationship with the disciples. People just don't allow you to wash
their feet. Some associates may think that you want something in return when they offer an act
of service or kindness, but Jesus shows us that we do well without anything in return. They
could never repay Jesus anyway, because He would give them the best gift of all time, which
is the promise of eternal life. It is there for all that choose to believe in Him, and why He died
for all of humanity.

Jesus demonstrates in this instance that we must never feel that we are above our
associates. He states in John 13:16, "A servant is never greater than his master, and the
messenger is not greater than the one who sent him." Jesus is letting us know that He is not
above God, and that He is willing to serve, because God sent Him to deliver the truth. He is a
servant of God, and those who have a supervisor are not greater than their supervisor and
should take wise counsel from them. Just as Jesus had to get on the same level as the disciples
by washing their feet, a leader, a supervisor, or a manager has to get on the same level as the
people, which strengthens the relationship in the workplace.

Jesus also sets a pattern in the home. Once when hanging out with Martha and Mary, Mary poured an expensive perfume on Jesus, and began scrubbing His feet with her hair. This gesture was an act of love, along with a great spiritual relationship with Jesus. Jesus often spent time with Martha, Mary, and Lazarus, and their fellowship is mentioned throughout the gospel. Jesus was there when Lazarus died, and He wept as well. He later brought Lazarus back from the dead. Jesus is showing us that relationships are important both in and out of the workplace. The disciples were like a family to Him. He saved them from fierce storms, and He continued to encourage them when they doubted. He also forgave them when they doubted Him as the rest of the world was crucifying Him.

#74: Jesus Sticks Closer Than a Brother

Some friends play at friendship but a true friend
sticks closer than one's nearest kin.
—Proverbs 18:24

A leader is known by the company that he associates with. Every leader needs a buddy or pal, and that person should be someone he can trust and respect wholeheartedly. First, the leader must have a relationship with God. A relationship is developed when we daily pray to God and confess our sins and ask God to direct every step of our life. We also seek our relationships in order to tell others about Jesus. King David had Jonathan as his best friend on earth and the brotherly friendship between the two was like no other friendship. Jonathan, son of Saul, could have spent all his energy on helping his own father remain as king or prepare himself to become king. Instead, he saw king potential in David and supported him through following God. He even told David that King Saul was plotting to kill David. He gave David his sword, and he was there for David.

We all need friends like Jonathan. It is rare to find a friend like him. Many leaders surround themselves with people that do not add value to them, which is a beginning of destruction. You have to pray and ask God who should be in your inner circle. Seek God first and He will be your best friend. It would also help to have a fellowship buddy or someone to whom you are accountable.

A friend is someone who will step on your shoes without messing up your shine, and remember that you must be supportive of your friend. Proverbs 28:6 says, "Better to be poor and walk in integrity than to be crooked in one's ways even though rich." Another saying that holds true to having a great friend or inner circle of friends is expressed in Proverbs 27:17, which says, "Iron sharpens iron, and one person sharpens the wits of another." A close friend will tell you when you are wrong, and will not worry about what you think. Proverbs 27:6 states, "Well meant are the wounds a friend inflicts, but profuse are the kisses of an enemy." Not everyone who comes across friendly is in your best interest. If your inner circle is fellows of God, then that is a good group of people who will add value to what you are trying to accomplish.

Last, not everyone who says he loves God really loves God. God warns us of the hypocrites. The best way to judge a person is by asking if he is walking a life with God. In Matthew 7:22-23, Jesus says, "Many will say to me on that day, 'Lord, Lord, did we not prophesy in your name, and in your name drive out demons and perform many miracles?' Then I will tell them plainly, 'I never knew you. Away from me, you evildoers!'" The company you keep is one of the most important decisions you can make. A 60-minute rule exists in open conversation. If someone doesn't credit God in some way in the first 60 minutes you meet them, then you may want to evaluate whether you want that person in your life. Are they drawing attention to themselves or willing to give to others? Every leader needs to be surrounded by a group of Jonathans, willing to serve and give up for their leader. Ultimately, we know that Jesus is closer to us than anyone in the human flesh, and He sticks closer than anyone.

#75: Not Easily Broken

*Two are better than one, because they have a good reward for
their toil. For if they fall, one will lift up the other; but woe to one
who is alone and falls and does not have another to help. Again, if
two lie together, they keep warm; but how can one keep warm
alone? And though one might prevail against another, two will
withstand one. A threefold cord is not quickly broken.*
—Ecclesiastes 4:9-12

Once, an elderly man, a younger boy, and a hunter were trapped in a cold place, and they were just about out of things to keep their self-started fire going. The elderly man had a collection of books with him, the hunter had a big fur coat, and the younger lad had a wooden box. After some time, they realized that in order to survive, someone would need to give up some items. The elderly man said, "I don't have much time left, and these books are worth a fortune. It will take care of my retirement. Let the lad throw in his wooden box." The younger lad said, "I have a collection of all the baseball cards over the last century in this box, and I am not going to throw my million in the fire. I think the hunter should throw in his big fur coat." The hunter explained, "I can keep warm in my fur coat alone. Why should I throw my stuff into the fire to keep you all warm?" Little did he know that the dropping temperatures in the night would be too much for the fur coat as well. If they had all thrown in their possessions, they would have lived, but they all perished. The moral of the story is that they didn't die from the cold without—they died from the cold within. Relationships require sacrifice, and if they had just stuck together, they would have survived.

In Ecclesiastes 4:9, God lets us know that two can succeed, and alone we can't accomplish anything. We need God in our lives first and foremost. With friends and healthy relationships, one person can help the other person when they fall. This fact is especially true in family relationships, team dynamics, and in the workplace. Once unity is formed, one person can look out for the other. The same is true in marital relationships, where both people lying together can keep each other warm. It requires giving not just material possessions to the other person, but sometimes just giving our time and showing that we care. In Ecclesiastes 3:1, God tells us, "For everything there is a season, a time for every activity under heaven." A time when we just need to listen, and a time when we need to speak up. A time to cry, and a time to laugh.

Ecclesiastes 4:12 talks about how three are better than one. In football or basketball, we cannot have a one-man show. Each athlete has to rely on the assistance of the team. In the same way, in a marriage, one party cannot dominate the relationship, and can't try to go it alone. God talks about the triple-braided cord, which represents the three people in the relationship. That third party is Jesus Christ. No relationship can survive without Jesus being a part of it. A marriage with Jesus as the third cord is impossible to separate, and that marriage can overcome any challenges.

#76: Martha's Cooking

Now as they went on their way, He entered a certain village, where a woman named Martha welcomed him into her home. She had a sister named Mary, who sat at the Lord's feet and listened to what He was saying. But Martha was distracted by her many tasks; so she came to him and asked, "Lord, do you not care that my sister has left me to do all the work by myself? Tell her then to help me." But the Lord answered her, "Martha, Martha, you are worried and distracted by many things; there is need of only one thing. Mary has chosen the better part, which will not be taken away from her."
—Luke 10:38-42

This situation happens to the best of us. Relatives are coming to town, and we get caught up in preparing them a place to sleep or cooking up a large meal. We check off all the places and events that we want to take them to, and we just stay on the go the entire time. Before you know it, we are driving them back to the airport, or they are pulling off in their rental vehicle. Then you say to yourself, "I really should have asked them more questions about their life and how they are doing." Sometimes, we miss the forest because of the many trees that are in the way.

Martha has the anxiety of family coming into town. Jesus is coming, so she is cooking, baking, and cleaning. She wants everything to be right for the Lord. But the other sister Mary is at Jesus' feet listening to the word of God. They both are friends of Jesus, but Martha is worried about the cares of this world. Martha even asks why Mary is not helping with the dinner. Jesus states to Martha that she is too wrapped up in the details. We need to ask ourselves what our details are. What distracts us on Sunday when it is time to go worship and grow? What is keeping us from developing a stronger prayer time with God? What is holding us back from being obedient? The world offers many distractions and details. In today's world, success is recognized as degrees, money, houses, cars, big families, etc. Like Mary, we need to be at Jesus' feet every moment we can, and listen to what He is telling us to do. We can do that daily by praying and reading the word of God.

The Bible also says that Martha was distracted by the big dinner that she was preparing. We can get distracted in the workplace. In sports, the coach may focus so much on the details of winning that he does not really develop a friendship or relationship with his team, which is more important. The coach may see the team as a commodity—a way to win so he can be promoted. The coach has to know the name of each athlete, and know what is going on in his athletes' lives. The coach needs to know if they are having financial or relationship difficulties and what is going on with them mentally and spiritually. Teaching technical skills will not be successful until the coach has connected emotionally and spiritually with the team. The coach's distractions may include practice, watching film, pregame planning, making travel arrangements, etc.

We have to remember what Jesus has shown us in dealing with Martha and Mary. We now know what is more important. We need to get at God's feet today by getting on our knees and praying out to God. We also need to get our priorities in order, and put God and serving his children first on our agenda.

12

Finances

#77: The Homecoming

Jesus continued: "There was a man who had two sons. The younger one said to his father, 'Father, give me my share of the estate.' So he divided his property between them. Not long after that, the younger son got together all he had, set off for a distant country, and there squandered his wealth in wild living. After he had spent everything, there was a severe famine in that whole country, and he began to be in need. So he went and hired himself out to a citizen of that country, who sent him to his fields to feed pigs. He longed to fill his stomach with the pods that the pigs were eating, but no one gave him anything.
—Luke 15:11-16

A lot of brother versus brother situations are referred to in the Bible. We saw the jealousy between Cain and Abel. Next, Jacob and Esau had conflicts with each other. Then Joseph was hated by his brothers. As we go further on, David was looked down upon by his brothers until he was anointed king. In some way, most of these conflicts dealt with inheritance and finance. Money has a way of turning families against each other, and in the story of the prodigal son, we see where one brother became jealous of the other brother because of the good treatment he received.

In Luke 15:11-16, we are able to see the heart of most teenagers, even in today's world. The one son demanded an early inheritance from his father, and he wanted to enjoy his life at that moment, instead of waiting until his father's death. It was not typical for a son to receive his inheritance early, especially since he was the younger son. The father went ahead and gave him his share of the money, and the younger son squandered the money in partying, prostitutes, and wild living. He hit rock bottom, and had to work in a pig pen. The son had done the typical thing, which was to waste all his funds because of insecurity and immaturity.

Later, the younger son came to his senses, and he realized that he would have a better living by going back home to live with his father. His father saw him coming, and began to shout with joy. He prepared a good meal for his son's homecoming, and he had a major celebration. The brother of the younger son showed envy, because his father had never done anything like that for him and he had not wasted his inheritance. Just like the father being happy of the younger son coming home, our Heavenly Father is happy when we come in from rebellion and financial trouble. At some time, just about everyone will go through a financial crisis, whether it is with credit cards, a mortgage, losing a job, or like the prodigal son, just overspending.

It is important to save for a rainy day. It is also important to honor God with our money. One son came back home to his blood father, but he also came back to God. He probably learned a lot from his bad habits in the streets. Sin results in consequences, and his wild living may have caused him to live a different life because he had used all of his savings up. The great thing is that he found his way back to the truth. God is teaching us through this story that it is important to live a disciplined life. He is teaching us that we have to handle our finances with care, and we have to rejoice when a brother comes home, instead of being envious when someone comes back home from sinning.

#78: Money Matters

A certain ruler asked Him, "Good teacher, what must I do to inherit eternal life?" "Why do you call me good?" Jesus answered. "No one is good, except God alone. You know the commandments: Do not commit adultery, do not murder, do not steal, do not give false testimony, honor your father and mother." "All these I have kept since I was a boy," he said. When Jesus heard this, he said to him, "You still lack one thing. Sell everything you have and give to the poor, and you will have treasure in heaven. Then come, follow me." When he heard this, he became very sad, because he was a man of great wealth.
—Luke 18:18-23

At some point, every successful person reaches the point that the rich, young ruler was at. He had acquired a lot in his lifetime. He was successful on his job, and he was respected in the community. He had a house, cars, and many material things. But he was still not fulfilled. Maybe he had tried to be a good person and follow the law. Many rich folks do great things for the community, and they give a lot of money away. They also follow good moral lives. But God requires something higher in order to acquire eternal life.

Ephesians 2:8 states, "It is grace that we are saved and not of ourselves." The rich, young ruler could do nothing in his own strength to gain eternal life. What happened in his life that made him think about where he would spend eternal life? After all, he had everything that money could buy. It was a good time in the life of the young ruler, because at least he was acquiring from Jesus what he needed to do. Obviously, the ruler was not fulfilled by all his money and fame, which could happen with success in any organization and with any individual.

The ruler is talking to the right person about his eternal state, and that person is Jesus Christ. His answer saddened the ruler, because Jesus told him to do three things: sell all his possessions, give to the poor, and follow Jesus. The Bible says that the ruler became sad, because he had a lot of possessions. The young fellow was faced with the truth, but he walked away from eternal life. He was not willing to give up the material things. He was not connected with serving God to the fullest, because he was not obedient to what Jesus had asked him to do.

What is God asking us to give up today? What is the one thing that is standing in the way of our eternal life? Have we given up everything for the Lord, and are we helping those who are less fortunate than us? Are we following after the heart of Jesus? Jesus served others throughout His entire ministry. Unlike this ruler, we can make a choice to release the things that are causing us not to be right with God. It is usually money that causes us to be not right with God. If it is a large house payment that is taking all of our funds, then maybe it is time to sell. If it is a large car payment, then it is time to release it. We may be hoarding our money like the one man was doing with grain, but like that man, you can't carry it with you. We need to examine what we need to release, who we can help, and if we are following the Lord with all of our heart.

#79: Three Strikes, You're Out

Jesus answered, "It is written: 'Man does not live on bread alone, but on every word that comes from the mouth of God.' Then the devil took Him to the holy city and had Him stand on the highest point of the temple. 'If you are the Son of God,' he said, 'throw yourself down. For it is written: He will command his angels concerning you, and they will lift you up in their hands, so that you will not strike your foot against a stone.' Jesus answered him, "It is also written: 'Do not put the Lord your God to the test.'" Again, the devil took him to a very high mountain and showed him all the kingdoms of the world and their splendor. "All this I will give you," he said, "if you will bow down and worship me." Jesus said to him, "Away from me, Satan! For it is written: 'Worship the Lord your God, and serve him only.'" Then the devil left Him, and angels came and attended Him.
—Matthew 4:4-11

The love of money has caused many to deviate from God. As a person runs after more money on the job, it means less time with the family and less quiet time with God. It is better to be content with what we have, and God tells us in His word that He will always provide enough. Another scripture said that a person cannot serve two masters. Luke 16:13 states, "No servant can serve two masters, either he will hate the one and love the other, or he will be devoted to the one and despise the other. You cannot serve both God and money." Of course the devil is part of the world, and he uses money as a way to pull others from their faith with God. He made an attempt at Jesus.

Jesus shows the devil and everyone else that He is truly the Son of God, and He is the one who will bring salvation to the world. Jesus was being tempted by the devil, and He had been fasting for 40 days and nights. Jesus had all the same feelings that we have, so after fasting for 40 days, He had to be hungry. The first thing the devil tempted Jesus with was food. Perhaps knowing that Jesus was hungry, the devil encouraged Him to turn stone into bread. Quickly, Jesus told the devil that man does not live on bread alone, but he lives on the word of God, which is how we have to deal with the evil one when we are being tempted to rebel against God. We have to remember the passage from Matthew 11:28 that states, "God does not put more on us that we can bare, and we have to cast our anxieties on God."

The devil then took Him to a high place in the Holy City and told Him, "If you are the Son of God, then throw yourself down." The devil used scripture, telling Jesus that God would save Him if He would throw Himself off of the high point. Jesus answered by telling him that we should not put the Lord God to the test. The devil offered Jesus all these material things, but Jesus was able to withstand the troubles that the devil was causing. We know that God can test and examine us, but we are taught not to test God. We are not to accept a bribe from anyone, and we are to be frugal with our resources so that we don't have to test God and see if He will bail us out.

Last, the devil took Jesus to another high place, and promised to give the city and land to Jesus only if He would bow down and serve him. Many people accept this bribe from the devil. It may not seem like it at the time, but running after more money or moving to a more comfortable situation may mean that we are not trusting God. Jesus let the devil know that we are to serve God and only God and He told the devil to get away. Jesus modeled how we are to deal with the temptations of the devil and how we are to handle status and money.

#80: Well Done, Good and Faithful Servant

The second came and said, 'Sir, your mina has earned five more.' His master answered, 'You take charge of five cities.' Then another servant came and said, 'Sir, here is your mina; I have kept it laid away in a piece of cloth. I was afraid of you, because you are a hard man. You take out what you did not put in and reap what you did not sow. His master replied, 'I will judge you by your own words, you wicked servant! You knew, did you, that I am a hard man, taking out what I did not put in, and reaping what I did not sow. Why then didn't you put my money on deposit, so that when I came back, I could have collected it with interest? Then he said to those standing by, 'Take his mina away from him and give it to the one who has ten minas.'
—Luke 19:18-24

Because of the economy, many people are afraid to invest their retirement and future funds in 401(k) and retirement plans. Some people have lost their entire savings, and a few banks have gone under in the past few years. These events show us that we can't put our trust in money alone, because money can come and go pretty fast. God shows us in the parable of the talents, that He expects us to save our money. We are not to live in fear but are to save an inheritance for our children's children. Proverbs 13:22-23 reads, "A good man leaves an inheritance for his children's children, but a sinner's wealth is stored up for the righteous. A poor man's field may produce abundant food, but injustice sweeps it away."

God expects us to save some of our money. We have to first remember that He provides it all, and He watches how we use our funds. In the parable of the talents, the first servant invested his mina and had 10 more by the time the master returned. He told him, "Well done, good and faithful servant." The second servant also invested his mina, and earned five more, and the master also said "Well done." But the third servant hid his mina away and did not invest it. Several reasons exist as to why he did not invest it: first, he may have thought he had plenty of time to grow the investment, so he kept living without saving; second, he may have failed to trust God with investing, so he kept it all for himself; and third, he may not have had the wisdom of investing.

God makes it clear that He wants us to save. Unlike the servant who did not invest, we have to invest our money. The minas or talents can also refer to investing in other lives, and God expects us to spread the gospel. It is not always just about money, but God is watching to see if we are planting seeds for the kingdom.

We need to think about the last time we prayed with someone or shared Jesus Christ with another person. We should also give to the poor, and provide tithes and offerings where we are serving. We invest in the kingdom of God by giving money and time away. We also invest in the kingdom by doing the will of God, and the return on that investment is extraordinary. We never know how far a kind word goes with another, but just by sharing the gospel, we know that it goes for eternity. We need to change our view on money today. Money is needed, but it is not everything. It is not too late to start saving. It is not too late to start sharing the good news with others. We need to start saving, and make the Father proud that we are building up an inheritance for our children's children.

#81: The Widow's Last

Elijah said to her, "Don't be afraid. Go home and do as you have said. But first, make a small cake of bread for me from what you have and bring it to me, and then make something for yourself and your son. For this is what the Lord, the God of Israel says: 'The jar of flour will not be used up and the jug of oil will not run dry until the day the Lord gives rain on the land.'" She went away and did as Elijah had told her. So there was food every day for Elijah and for the woman and her family. For the jar of flour was not used up and the jug of oil did not run dry, in keeping with the word of the Lord spoken by Elijah.
—1 Kings 17:13

The widow was on her last bit of flour in a jar, and she only had a little oil. Elijah the Prophet came in to the widow's presence, and he asked her for something to eat along with something to drink. She said that she had planned to eat this last bit, and she and her son were planning to die. 1 Kings 17:12 states, "As surely as the Lord your God lives," she replied, "I don't have any bread, only a handful of flour in a jar and a little oil in a jug. I am gathering a few sticks to take home and make a meal for myself and my son that we may eat it and die." This lady was preparing her own last supper, then a prophet came, asking her for her last meal. How would you have responded?

The widow was obedient to the prophet, and she prepared the meal for Elijah. She had to obey the prophet first in order to keep herself and her son alive. As she obeyed, her flour and oil were never fully consumed. God took care of her, because she took care of the prophet. This pattern is one for all of us to follow. Even when we are low on resources, we should bless the church and the prophet. It comes down to a trust issue. Are we going to trust what we can do with it, or are we going to trust what God is going to do with the funds? Malachi 3:10 states, "Bring the whole tithe into the storehouse, that there may be food in my house. Test me in this," says the Lord Almighty, "and see if I will not throw open the floodgates of heaven and pour out so much blessing that you will not have room enough for it." But in order to receive this blessing, God is watching to see if we do what the widow did with her limited resources.

In a similar situation, another poor widow gave everything she had to God. Luke 21:1-4 states, "As He looked up, Jesus saw the rich putting their gifts into the temple treasury. He also saw a poor widow put in two very small copper coins. 'I tell you the truth,' He said, 'this poor widow has put in more than all the others. All these people gave their gifts out of their wealth; but she out of her poverty put in all she had to live on.'"

The word of God tells us to give at least 10 percent of our earnings back to God. Just remember it is all the Lord's, and it is important that we manage the other 90 percent well, which is what God's living word teaches us to do. It teaches us how to save for our children's children. It teaches us to sell all our possessions, and give to the poor. It teaches us to store our riches in heaven where moths and rust cannot destroy them. It teaches us to do as the widows have done—and we have to be willing to give it all up for the Lord. We need to think about what we are giving back to the Lord and what we are piling up. What in our house can be destroyed by moths and rust? The word also says the debtor is a slave to the lender. We need to free ourselves from debt, because it is not the will of God for our life.

#82: No Crossing Over

There was a rich man who was dressed in purple and fine linen and lived in luxury every day. At his gate was laid a beggar named Lazarus, covered with sores and longing to eat what fell from the rich man's table. Even the dogs came and licked his sores. The time came when the beggar died and the angels carried him to Abraham's side. The rich man also died and was buried. In hell, where he was in torment, he looked up and saw Abraham far away, with Lazarus by his side. So he called to him, "Father Abraham, have pity on me and send Lazarus to dip the tip of his finger in water and cool my tongue, because I am in agony in this fire." But Abraham replied, "Son, remember that in your lifetime you received your good things, while Lazarus received bad things, but now he is comforted here and you are in agony. And besides all this, between us and you a great chasm has been fixed, so that those who want to go from here to you cannot, nor can anyone cross over from there to us."
—Luke 16:19-26

When the ball game is over, you can't go back and change the outcome of the game. You can only reflect back: What if the team had made that play? What if we had tried a little harder? This scenario is much the same way as it will be in the end of time. Many people will look back and say, "Only if I had walked right during the time in my life." The rich man and Lazarus are as real as the living word can get, and it makes us all think about where we want to spend eternity. As we look back on the rich, young ruler, he may very well be the same guy who is now being tormented because he failed to sell all his possessions, give to the poor, and follow Jesus Christ.

Where do you want to spend eternity? Although the beggar went without during his lifetime, he ended up with the prize possession. He ended up with the highest honor that can come from living on this earth, and that honor is spending eternity with God Almighty. The rich man went to hell, but Lazarus the beggar went to heaven. All the money and splendor could not buy the rich man eternal life. Nothing is run with money; it's what we do with it once God gives it to us. Lazarus is rejoicing today, and if he could testify to us, he would probably say that it is hard here on earth, but struggling is well worth the prize. He would probably say to us, you can trust Jesus Christ with your life. He would tell us to hold on and endure during the roughest times.

Another rich man who was very wealthy began to pile up his savings. Luke 12:18-21 says, "Then he said, 'This is what I'll do. I will tear down my barns and build bigger ones, and there I will store all my grain and my goods. And I'll say to myself, 'You have plenty of good things laid up for many years. Take life easy; eat, drink, and be merry.' But God said to him, 'You fool! This very night your life will be demanded from you. Then who will get what you have prepared for yourself?' This is how it will be with anyone who stores up things for himself but is not rich toward God.'" This passage says it all. The rich ruler is just like everyone else in the world. The more money that flows in, a tendency exists to want *more* money to flow in. We are seeing clearly that the love of money truly is a root to all evil in mankind. We have to be prepared for the Lord at all times, and we have to be good stewards over the finances that God has given us. We need to give God not just our money and tithes, but we also must give Him our time. God tells us again in 1 Samuel 15:22 that obedience is better than sacrifice.

13

Thinking

#83: Reflecting Forward

And now, dear brothers and sisters, one final thing. Fix your thoughts on what is true, and honorable, and right, and pure, and lovely, and admirable. Think about things that are excellent and worthy of praise.
—Philippians 4:8

We all spend many hours every day getting ready for work or school. We organize our clothes, food, and supplies for the day. We make sure our car has enough gas in it. When it comes to serving God, we get our church time in, and we also work in fellowship. We spend time praying and worshiping God. However, we tend to fall short in one area, and that is reflecting and thinking. We may do a lot of reading, but how much are we thinking and reflecting on what we are reading or experiencing in our life? In Genesis, it says on the seventh day, God took a rest from what He did, and after each day, He would say "and it was good." In order to make a statement like that, He had to look back on the day, and see the beauty of His work accomplished. God also was able to notice that it was not good for man to be alone, so He created woman. He may have been looking down at the world, and saw that it was good.

How much time do you spend thinking and reflecting? In Philippians 4:8, the scripture tells us to fix our thoughts on those things that are true, honorable, right, pure, lovely, and admirable. In other words, God is telling us to focus on the positive things in life. The word "fix" in Webster's dictionary means to make fast, firm, and stable. Other verses in the Bible relate to being fixed. One verse is in Hebrews 12:2, which states, "Let us fix our eyes on Jesus, the author and perfecter of our faith, who for the joy set before Him, endured the cross, scorning its shame, and sat down at the right hand of the throne of God." As long as we stay constantly fixed on Jesus, then our thoughts will be focused on positive things. The most honorable and admirable task to accomplish in this life is to one day be told by the Father, "Well done," and to receive a one-way ticket to heaven. When we fix our eyes on Jesus, many of the great qualities in Philippians 4:8 become evident.

The last part of this verse states that we should think on things that are excellent and praiseworthy. We know that no one ever walked this earth and lived an excellent life except Jesus Christ himself. And because of that, we owe Him all our praise and worship. He was the only one who was without sin, and only became human to die for our sins, and give us an opportunity for salvation. We can never be perfect like Christ (Matthew 5:48), but as long as we are fixed on Him, we are doing the excellent thing. We must praise Him at every opportunity that permits. Thinking about things that are not good will only bring heartache and a bad attitude. We have a choice whether to look at life through foggy lenses, or we can see the good in every opportunity. Jesus is worthy of the praise, because He gave us a gift that we can never pay back—He died for us. It is praiseworthy to give Him praise, and it is praiseworthy to confess and repent our sins. It is praiseworthy to pray to the Lord, and to meditate on God's word day and night. All these deeds are noble and honorable. We cannot do anything in our strength to receive all the gifts, except give God the honor and praise for allowing us to stay healthy.

#84: Wise Thinking

"Now, O Lord my God, you have made your servant king in place of my father David. But I am only a little child and do not know how to carry out my duties. Your servant is here among the people you have chosen, a great people, too numerous to count or number. So give your servant a discerning heart to govern your people and to distinguish between right and wrong. For who is able to govern this great people of yours?" The Lord was pleased that Solomon had asked for this. So God said to him, "Since you have asked for this and not for long life or wealth for yourself, nor have asked for the death of your enemies but for discernment in administering justice, I will do what you have asked. I will give you a wise and discerning heart, so that there will never have been anyone like you, nor will there ever be. Moreover, I will give you what you have not asked for—both riches and honor—so that in your lifetime you will have no equal among kings."
—1 Kings 3:7-13

If you had three wishes from God what would you ask for? Some people would ask for enough food and money for a lifetime. Other people may ask for a dream home or a certain status on the job. Proverbs 1:7 says, "The fear of the Lord is the beginning of knowledge, but fools despise and discipline." In order for us to have a great thinking life, we need to ask God for wisdom. Solomon asked God for wisdom above all other things. He asked for the best thing, because with wisdom, he would be able to lead people. We can read many books and go to many conferences, but true discernment and how to govern comes from God, and we have to fear God to receive this wisdom.

We gain wisdom when we turn our life totally over to God. Proverbs 16:9 states, "In his heart a man plans his course, but the Lord determines his steps." We have to be on God's agenda in order to know how to complete our own plan. God knows our deepest thoughts, and it is better to get counsel from Him even before we think about what is right and wrong. Before we make plans, we should ask God for discernment, and one way to receive this discernment is through reading of the word. God's word has a solution to every problem that life throws at us. Another scripture that speaks along the same lines of asking God for understanding is Psalm 127:1, which states, "Unless the Lord builds the house, its builders labor in vain." Many businesses have been established in a year, but they soon close their doors because of poor service or financial trouble. Like Solomon, the earlier we can get involved in the thinking process, the safer our decisions will be in life.

Solomon wanted discernment so he would know right from wrong. He was given incredible wisdom from God, but he made many mistakes throughout his reign. God still referred to him as the greatest and richest king of all time. Solomon had many wives, and these women pulled him away from God's will. He wrote the book of Proverbs, and he became one of the wisest and richest kings of all time. With high positions come high expectations. He also built the temple for God, and many people were blessed during his reign as king. We can learn from Solomon that we must first ask God for wisdom, and once God honors that request, we must continue to be obedient and faithful to God's commands. Wisdom without fear equals great ability, but it also equals a weak character.

#85: The More You Know, the More Is Required

"But the one who does not know and does things deserving punishment will be beaten with few blows. From everyone who has been given much, much will be demanded; and from the one who has been entrusted with much, much more will be asked."
—Luke 12:48

It is an amazing thing to watch little kids grow up. They become adults right in front of our eyes, and we play an important role in showing them the right way to go. In Proverbs 22:6, the Bible tells us to train children in the way they should go, and they will never turn away from it. We have to give the knowledge of discipline, in the same way God gives His children knowledge and discipline. He is merciful and graceful, even when we go astray. Little kids can be devious, and we sometimes laugh at them when they do things contrary. For example, a little child can go in the food cabinets and open up a bag of flour and pour it all over the house and we may laugh at him. But when a child is grown up, and he leaves dishes on the table or in his bedroom, we are not so happy. The reason is because they should know better. In the same manner, God looks at us before we accept Jesus Christ as our Lord and Savior, and He perhaps looks away at our earlier mistakes because we don't know any better. Once we accept Christ as our Lord and Savior, God requires more of us and we may be disciplined for our actions.

Jesus once got away from his parents, and almost a whole day passed before they knew that He was missing. He had slipped away from them, and went and spent time in the temple. It took them three days to find Him, which is symbolic to Him rising on the third day. Jesus was sitting in the temple courts listening to the teaching of the Pharisees, and the Bible says that everyone who heard him was amazed at his wisdom. Luke 2:48-50 says, "When his parents saw Him, they were astonished. His mother said to him, 'Son, why have you treated us like this? Your father and I have been anxiously searching for you.' 'Why were you searching for me?' He asked. 'Didn't you know that I had to be in my Father's house? But they did not understand what he was saying to them.'" Most kids would have maybe received a spanking for slipping away, but Jesus was in the church when they found him. He was definitely different than any other child that has come along.

After we grow up, God and others expect more of us—when much is given, much is required. An airplane pilot is entrusted with the lives of thousands of people as they fly daily around the country. A quarterback or captain of the team is entrusted with a major part of the team's success. The captain or leader must set a pattern for everyone else, and more will be required of him. As we grow in our faith with God, He will add more value and people to our circle of influence—when much is given, much is required. The stronger our faith, the more people will join hands in our road to success. God sees our heart, and when we are pure, He will entrust more and more people to us in the area of leadership. We can't look back and think that we have wasted time. We need to begin this journey of leadership. God knows what state each one of us in, and He calls us to lead where we are. He will equip us with what we need to be a leader. We need to take Jesus' torch, which is all that is required to grow as a leader. The word of God is the mantle we need to go forth and spread the good and great news of Jesus Christ being our King.

#86: Combating Depressive Thoughts

Now Ahab told Jezebel everything Elijah had done and how he had killed all the prophets with the sword. So Jezebel sent a messenger to Elijah to say, "May the gods deal with me, be it ever so severely, if by this time tomorrow I do not make your life like that of one of them. Elijah was afraid and ran for his life. When he came to Beersheba in Judah, he left his servant there, while he himself went a day's journey into the desert. He came to a broom tree, sat down under it, and prayed that he might die. "I have had enough, Lord," he said. "Take my life; I am no better than my ancestors." Then, he lay down under the tree and fell asleep. All at once an angel touched him and said, "Get up and eat." He looked around, and there by his head was a cake of bread baked over hot coals, and a jar of water. He ate and drank and then lay down again.
—1 Kings 19:1-4

At some point, depression affects everyone and it all boils down to the thought life of the person. It also is a matter of what a person dwells on the most. If a person perceives bad things happening to him, it is almost certain to happen that way. Depression can move in after a period of success and a major setback or failure happens. We saw this scenario with the prophet Elijah. He had just won a major battle on Mount Carmel and he had received God's favor by defeating Ahab. All the people met at Mount Carmel to watch this great battle between the prophets. A famine and drought was in the land, and both men were going to call on their gods to have fire fall to burn the bull sacrifices that they had prepared. On that day, Elijah won because he relied on the Almighty God. He defeated Ahab and his 450 prophets of Baal, because when he prayed, God sent fire from heaven and burned up the sacrifice that he had prepared. The people of the land witnessed this event, and they followed Ahab.

Jezebel received word from Ahab of what Elijah did, and she sent a threatened message to Elijah that she would kill him. Elijah ran for his life because he was scared. 1 Kings 19:4 talks about how he just wanted to die. He was in an obvious depression. How could he fall in such a depression after a major victory on Mount Carmel? The Bible says that pride comes before destruction, but nothing was prideful about what Elijah did. The angel woke him up, and fed him. God eventually asked Elijah why he was running, and He told him to go back the way that he came.

That course is the only way out of depression. You have to start doing the things you used to do. You have to start working out again, and you have to keep positive people in your company. You have to keep believing in yourself, and you have to stay active in mind and body. By reading God's word, you will remove the negative thoughts and replace them with encouragement. During depression, a person's faith is weakened, but fellowship with others is crucial in getting that person to believe in himself again. Philippians 3:13-14 states, "Brothers, I do not consider myself yet to have taken hold of it. But one thing I do: Forgetting what is behind and straining toward what is ahead, I press on toward the goal to win the prize for which God has called me heavenward in Christ Jesus." The one thing that Elijah was doing during his depression was praying. As long as you stay connected to God, you have a way out.

#87: Delighting in God's Playbook Defeats Depression

Blessed is the man who does not walk in the counsel of the wicked or stand in the way of sinners or sit in the seat of mockers. But his delight is in the law of the Lord, and on his law he meditates day and night. He is like a tree planted by streams of water, which yields its fruit in season and whose leaf does not wither. Whatever he does prospers. Not so the wicked! They are like chaff that the wind blows away. Therefore the wicked will not stand in the judgment, nor sinners in the assembly of the righteous. For the Lord watches over the way of the righteous, but the way of the wicked will perish.
—Psalm 1:1-6

As coaches and athletes, we have to follow the rules of the game, and we also have to follow the rules of the organization. Just recently, the University of Alabama had to forfeit over 20 games, because student athletes were illegally using scholarship book money to help other athletes. Some of the athletes who have tampered with steroids are losing their integrity, and they are gaining a lifetime of shame from breaking the rules. The choices we make have consequences, and most people feel that they will never get caught. They may start out just cheating a little, or just using a little of a supplement. Cracks in a person's character are usually escalated unless they are brought under check.

God teaches us in Psalm 1:1 that a person is blessed when he does not walk in the counsel of the wicked, stand in the way of sinners, or sit in the seat of mockers. We need to read God's word, and make sure that everything that we are doing and saying lines up with the will of our Father. If we don't know the rulebook, then that is different. But everyone has an opportunity to find out what God expects of them by reading the word of God. God is telling us today to walk an upright life, and we must not do what the sinners do. We can't cheat on taxes, take illegal drugs, or follow the patterns of nonbelievers that do not line up with what is in the Holy Bible.

We can receive joy by meditating on the word both day and night, which basically means that we need to be in touch with God throughout the day. Even a few hours without God's word can cause us to grow weary because of the pull of the world on our faith and belief. Psalm 1:2 tells us to meditate both day and night. We should come up with a reading plan that allows studying and meditating two to three times a day. Meditating is different than just reading the word. Meditation means we are going to read and set aside time to understand more fully what God is saying to us. We should look for ways to live out the commandments and other things God wants us to do. We need to diligently seek for the truth, and have a yearning for the love of God.

God says that through meditation of the word that we will be prosperous. For example, if a tree is planted by a stream, then that tree will grow and prosper because its roots can feed off of the stream for eternity. The wicked are compared to chaffs that are blown away, and the wicked will not stand in judgment. The great thing is that we know that God is always watching what we are doing, and He watches over the righteous. It is clearly stated that the way of the wicked leads to destruction. God wants us to go in the right direction, and the only way to do that is through prayer, studying, and meditating on God's word daily.

#88: Defeated Thinking

Early the next morning, Abraham took some food and a skin of water and gave them to Hagar. He set them on her shoulders and then sent her off with the boy. She went on her way and wandered in the desert of Beersheba. When the water in the skin was gone, she put the boy under one of the bushes. Then she went off and sat down nearby about a bowshot away, for she thought, "I cannot watch the boy die." And as she sat there nearby, she began to sob. God heard the boy crying and the angel of God called to Hagar from heaven and said to her, "What is the matter, Hagar? Do not be afraid; God has heard the boy crying as he lies there. Lift the boy up and take him by the hand, for I will make him into a great nation." Then God opened her eyes and she saw a well of water. So she went and filled the skin with water and gave the boy a drink.
—Genesis 21:14-19

Sometimes in a ball game, we see no way out. When the other team is batting, they just continue to run the score up. The other team has all the superstars, and we just can't get a break. We should never give up in life, no matter how bad the circumstances are. We are fighting an enemy, but we have the power to defeat this enemy. A coach will bring in a relief pitcher if the starting pitcher becomes tired and weary. The football coach will bring in the second or third string. We have Jesus Christ, who is always ready to assist us in fighting the enemy. We have something deep down in our soul, which gives us the ability to fight the devil. We have the Holy Spirit. 1 John 4:4 says, "You, dear children, are from God and have overcome them, because the one who is in you is greater than the one who is in the world." Jesus has already defeated the devil, and He is on the battleground tired and defeated. We have to remember that. When Jesus Christ rose from the dead, He silenced the powers of the devil forever. The devil only has power if we give him power. With prayer, meditation, and using the word of God against the devil, we are victorious.

Hagar had been cashed out. She was the maidservant of Sarah, and because Sarah was barren for a while, she gave her husband Abraham to Hagar so that they could produce a child. Once the child was born, Sarah became envious of both the newborn son Ishmael and Hagar. Eventually, Abraham asked Hagar and Ishmael to leave. He gave them some water and food, and basically put them in the street. Hagar was defeated. The word of God says that after all the water ran out, she placed her son Ishmael under a tree and began to cry. But God heard her cry and he spoke to her from heaven to let her know that He would make Ishmael into a great nation. At that point, her eyes were opened, and she was able to see more water.

When we reach the state that Hagar is in, sometimes crying is good. God sees our tears, and He sends an angel. An angel comforted Hagar, and we have Jesus Christ to comfort us. All we have to do is pray and continue to read the word. We are comforted, and the water does not run out. We are able to get past the financial wars, relationship problems, work problems, family problems, and other bends of the truth.

#89: Delightful Thinking

For I delight in your commands because I love them. I lift up my hands to your commands, which I love, and I meditate on your decrees. Remember your word to your servant, for you have given me hope. My comfort is in my suffering is this: Your promise preserves my life. The arrogant mock me without restraint, but I do not turn from your law.
—Psalm 119:47

This thing called life is hard to manage. We have to figure out a way to make a living. We have to work with people that we don't really know. We have to manage our finances in a way to save for retirement, and at the same time leave an inheritance for our children and grandchildren. In athletics, we are battling a drug crisis with steroids. We are not really sure who is natural anymore. Many people do not fear God anymore, and they are doing anything they want to their bodies. Everyone needs to slow down, and spend more time reading and meditating on God's word. Going to church is just not enough. The preacher can give a good sermon and pump everyone up like a coach would do, but that wears off by Sunday night. This situation needs to change.

We need to meditate on God's word day and night as the Bible instructs us to do so. Psalm 37:4 says, "Take delight in the Lord, and He will give your heart's desires. Commit everything you do to the Lord. Trust Him, and He will help you." In order to take delight in the Lord, we must have a committed prayer life. We must also have a spiritual-growth plan where we are committed to learning about God. The only way to do that is to read and study God's word daily, and make a lifetime commitment in the process. Our lives merely change overnight when we commit all our thoughts and actions to God, and our faith is also increased through relationships with others. In Proverbs 27:17, the scripture says that iron sharpens iron as one brother sharpens another. We can encourage one another and instruct one another in God's word, which also helps our relationship with God.

We must continue to do what lines up with God's word, even when colleagues, friends, and family are going astray. God tells us in Matthew 7:13-14, "You can enter God's Kingdom only through the narrow gate. The highway to hell is broad, and its gate is wide for the many who choose that way. But the gateway to life is very narrow and the road is difficult and only a few ever find it." It is our duty to find out how God would have us live, and the way to do that is reading and studying the word. Narrow paths are hard to find. It is easier to play video games than to take a solid hour and read and pray. Psalm 48 says that we need to honor and love God's commands. Anything against the Lord is rebellion and sin. We do have a forgiving God, and that is why He sent His only begotten Son Jesus Christ to us, so He could redeem us from eternal death. Through Jesus Christ, we now have hope and victory. We still have to contend with the devil on a daily and hourly basis. Therefore, reading the word and praying will assure us of our continued victory journey.

We need to ask ourselves what our prayer life is like at the moment. We need to start spending time studying what God's word is saying. It opens new windows and fresh insight in God's love and purpose for our lives will be inevitable. We need to renew our prayer life and restore a passion to learn God's instructions.

14

Protection

#90: Working Behind the Scenes

Finally, be strong in the Lord and in His mighty power. Put on the full armor of God so that you can take your stand against the devil's schemes. For our struggle is not against flesh and blood, but against the rulers, against the authorities, against the powers of this darkness world, and against the spiritual forces of evil in the heavenly realms.
—Ephesians 6:10-12

When we go to see a movie, we rarely think of everything that has gone into making the movie. A lot goes on behind the scenes: casting, producing, sound, lighting, set design, editing, etc. In the same manner, God is fighting a lot of our battles behind the scene. Like a movie script, God is intercepting and filtering out the many schemes of the devil, so we can walk upright against him in human form. Many things exist that we are protected against, and we will never know how many fiery dots have been overturned by God. If we don't think that a spiritual battle is going on, we can go back to the conversation that God and the devil had regarding Job.

In Job 1:9-11, Satan says to God, "Does Job fear God for nothing? … Have you not put a hedge around him and his household and everything he has? You have blessed the work of his hands, so that his flocks and herds are spread throughout the land. But stretch out your hand and strike everything he has, and he will surely curse you to your face." Satan was saying that Job served God because of his material possessions. God gave the devil permission to attack Job, and told him that he could take everything except Job's life. In Job 1:12, "The Lord said to Satan, 'Very well, then, everything he has is in your hands, but on the man himself do not lay a finger.'" Isn't it awesome that the devil can do nothing without God's permission? This story is an example of the behind the scenes stuff that goes on that we don't know about, but the good thing is that God is in control of what happens both on earth and in the spiritual realm.

God gives us many weapons to help us fight the evil one. We know that we are not fighting against other humans, but it may very well be the evil spirits operating in others that we are fighting against. We have to put on our armor that God provides, and we have to take our stand against the spirits operating in others and against the devil himself. We have to pray for those who persecute us and feed the enemy at times. God tells us to pray for our enemies, and bless those who curse us. It is great to know that only God has control over our physical and our spiritual bodies.

#91: I've Got the Championship Belt

Therefore put on the full armor of God, so that when the day of evil
comes, you may be able to stand your ground, and after you have
done everything, to stand. Stand firm then, with the belt of truth buckled
around your waist, with the breastplate of righteousness in place.
—Ephesians 6:13-14

When going into competition, the athlete must have all of his gear well secured. In order to stand firm in competition, the athlete must have his shoes on well secured. In the sport of baseball, he must wear a helmet when receiving pitches. In any position, he must stand firm on the defense, not letting the ball get by him in any circumstance. The great thing is that eight other players are on the field as well. All the players back each other up if one misses the ball. In the same way, we have God to back us up if we make an error in the field. When getting dressed for competition, one of the most important items is securing the waistline with some form of a belt. In order to stand firm against the enemy, the Bible refers several times to the importance of tucking the uniform inside of the belt. One example is given in 1 Kings 18:46, which states, "The power of the Lord came upon Elijah and, tucking his cloak into his belt, he ran ahead of Ahab all the way to Jezreel."

God asks us to put on our full armor of God. In a real sense, it is easy to forget the belt around the waist. The minute a person gets to work and realizes that he has forgotten his belt, he immediately feels uneasy and self-conscious. At that point, it is hard to stand firm as the Bible instructs. It is hard to keep your shirt or top tucked in, and it is hard to keep your pants up. The belt symbolizes truth, and it must always be in place. Psalm 109:19 says, "May it be like a cloak wrapped about him, like a belt tied forever around him." Before we can do anything, we have to have on the belt of truth. All other parts of the gear will stay in place when the belt is secured at the center of the body. Paul names the belt in the full armor of God, which also indicates the significance of holding on to the truth. We must always hold on to the truth.

Before the people went on a long journey, God gave the importance of the belt in the Passover. Exodus 12:11 states, "This is how you are to eat it: with your cloak tucked into your belt, your sandals on your feet and your staff in your hand. Eat it in haste; it is the Lord's Passover." The belt again symbolizes the truth, and truth comes from reading the word of God, the Holy Bible. John 8:32 says, "The truth will set you free."

Before going into any battle it is important to ask ourselves if we are ready for battle. We also need to ask ourselves if God is in this thing that we are fighting for. We must have our belt on every day for battle. Matthew 3:4 describes John the Baptist's attire, stating, "John's clothes were made of camel's hair, and he had a leather belt around his waist. His food was locust and honey." John didn't have many clothes, but his belt was so important that it was made of leather. We must buckle up every day with the truth, which will secure the rest of our gear. The sword is held in place by the belt, and the other garments are all secured by the belt of truth. The truth comes from studying and meditating on God's word. Daniel 10:5 says, "I looked up and there before me was a man dressed in linen, with a belt of the finest gold around his waist." God's word is as powerful as the finest gold, and we must stay buckled up and stand firm with His word.

#92: Is Your Heart Guarded?

Stand firm then, with the belt of truth buckled around your waist,
with the breastplate of righteousness in place.
—Ephesians 6:14

The breastplate or corselet was usually made up of two parts and protected the body on both sides, from the neck to the middle. The Bible uses it metaphorically with the term righteousness. When going into battle, it is important to have the midsection of your body protected. Many officers will wear a bulletproof vest to protect against the enemy. All of our most vital organs are at the midline of our body, and one of the main organs is our heart. The enemy will definitely go for that area first. In the book *The Hobbit*, the big dragon was only vulnerable in one place, which was the area around the heart that was uncovered. Bard was able to slay the dragon by hitting him with an arrow in the heart, because the once invincible dragon failed to cover its heart.

In sports, such as baseball and softball, the catchers have to use the guard in order to protect themselves from being hit in the midsection by the ball. Football players often wear pads to protect the sternum and chest area. In the sports world, you rarely see any equipment on the back side of a person. But God protects the front and the back with the breastplate of righteousness. We rarely run from our enemies or against an opponent, but the enemy that we are fighting is the devil. Just as in football, the devil will hit you from behind or clip you. He doesn't care how you fall as long as you fall. But God has given us protection with the breastplate, and it guards our heart from the fiery dots of the enemy from the back and the front.

The breastplate definitely symbolizes righteousness. Isaiah 59:17 says, "He put on righteousness as his breastplate, and the helmet of salvation on his head; he put on garments of vengeance and wrapped himself in zeal as in a cloak." Isaiah 9:7 talks about Jesus Christ being the true upholder of righteousness. The passage says, "Of the increase in government and peace there will be no end. He will reign on David's throne and over his kingdom, establishing and upholding it with justice and righteousness from that time on and forever. The zeal of the Lord Almighty will accomplish this." As long as we have Jesus Christ in our life, this breastplate is the entire armor that is needed. We know that Jesus is the only right way to salvation. Through Jesus Christ we can know God.

If we know Christ, then we have the breastplate of righteousness on as part of our armor. We need the breastplate to protect us from Satan. Jesus Christ covers the heart, and He lets us know what is right. In John 14:6 Jesus answered, "I am the way and the truth and the life. No one comes to the Father except through me." Jesus instructs us what true righteousness is. It is not necessarily by obeying the law, where we can receive salvation. It is recognizing Jesus as the only way to get right with God. In order to get to God, we have to go through Jesus, which is the one major thing to remember when we are revealing our hearts to God and others. We must put on our breastplate, and make sure that we have thanked God for the ultimate breastplate, Jesus Christ. We can stand firm knowing that we have the best armor of all, and it can handle any darts thrown by the enemy. Our hearts are not wide open unless we have accepted Jesus Christ as our Lord and savior.

#93: Carrying the Message First Class

"…and with your feet fitted with the readiness
that comes from the gospel of peace."
—Ephesians 6:15

I never thought that I would see the day where a regular pair of tennis shoes would reach over $150.00. In today's stores, a pair of training shoes can easily cost over that price. Our shoes are important in the sense that they carry us everywhere we need to go. People tend to look down to see what type of shoes you have on. Many people judge a person by his shoes. A pastor once said that you can tell the state of a person just by looking at his shoes. If a person's shoes are old and worn down, it may be an indication that the person is worn down. The poem *Footprints* relates how, in a dream, a man saw two sets of footprints on the sands of life along the beach throughout most of his life, but only one set of footprints during the worst periods of his lifetime. Selfishly, he asked God, "Where were you during these lonely times in my life?" In the story, God says, "My dear child, it was then that I carried you."

We need to ask ourselves what we are carrying with us each morning that our feet hit the floor. Are we carrying a personal message of our own testimony, or are we using this testimony to help and bless other people? In Ephesians 6:15, a part of our armor consists of fitting our feet "with the readiness that comes from the gospel of peace." If we are looking from an athletic standpoint, this armor is the offense against the devil. Most of the armor deals with personal protection against the works of the enemy, but we can get on the offense by telling others about the armor and, more importantly, telling them about Jesus Christ. One of our missions daily is as long as God is allowing our feet to hit the floor, we can make a promise that we are going to share the good news with everyone we come in contact with each day. In this manner, we are putting armor on others, such as our families, friends, and working colleagues. We just have to tell them about Jesus, and how important it is that we use the God-given armor to help us fight the works of the enemy.

Jesus lays the groundwork when it comes to setting an example of getting our feet ready for transporting the gospel. One significant thing that He did was wash the feet of the disciples. When a man's feet are clean, the whole body is clean. Jesus was preparing the disciples for ministry that day, and He also showed us that we must stay humble and provide leadership through washing the feet of others. Equivalent to walking with God and being ready, we need to ask ourselves who the last person was that we attempted to lead to Jesus Christ.

If God grants us the power to get out of bed in the morning, then we must give the entire day back to Him. We can also ask God for a divine appointment every day as we go ready with the word of the Lord. 2 Timothy 2:15 says, "Do your best to present yourself to God as one approved by him, a worker who has no need to be ashamed, rightly explaining the word of truth." We must keep the Bible hidden away in our hearts, which is the will of God. In order to be used by God, we have to pray, read, and be full of an attitude to serve and help others like Jesus did in washing the feet of others.

#94: The Ultimate Shield

In addition to all this, take up the shield of faith, with which you
can extinguish all the flaming arrows of the evil one.
—Ephesians 6:16

The sport of dodge ball, where everyone is trying to hit their opponent with the ball, really has no protection. In baseball, the pitcher hurls close to a 100 mph cylinder only inches away from the batter. In the sports of boxing and mixed martial arts, the only real protection of the body is hands used as guards against getting hit. In any case, these individuals are taking major risks as they trust that their opponent will not intentionally try to hurt them. This case is not so with the devil. The devil throws to kill, or the devil throws with the intention to hurt someone. The devil does not care that you are hurting. An athlete takes a chance every time he steps up to the plate. Just as in football, when the contact from another player can be devastating, especially if the person is hit from behind through clipping or tackling below the knee. A lot of equipment is worn in football, because of the impact from others and ground force of falling down.

God provides us with the necessary equipment to protect us from Satan. God first handles the spiritual battle that is taking placed behind the scenes. He next provides us with the belt of truth, which comes from reading God's word. We also have the breastplate of righteousness, and we learned that our feet are used to deliver the gospel.

In theory, we can see that the first two weapons serve as defense mechanisms to help defend ourselves from the devil, but the fourth portion of armor, i.e., covering the feet with the gospel, gives us offense against the devil. Next, we have the shield of faith. In Ephesians 6:16, some Bibles say "above all" to start out the scripture, meaning that this weapon of faith may be the most important one. A shield is used to prevent the enemy from attacking us head on. The great thing about faith is that as it increases, our confidence increases. As we draw closer to God, He draws closer to us. The shield of faith is used symbolically with faith. Years ago in baseball, the players had a very small glove to catch the ball. When you look at the modern-day gloves, they are very large compared to what was used 50 years ago. The player's success in catching the ball has increased. In the same way, as we increase our faith, we feel more secure in dealing with the devil. We are willing to take more risks. We are not thrown by the evil temptations and evil schemes that are done by the devil. We are able to "above all" defeat the devil with every working step.

The shields used back in Roman soldier fighting days were very tall, almost as tall as a door. They were set up to totally block out all the fiery darts shot by the enemy. The shields were large enough to cover the entire body of the soldiers. Ephesians 6:16 states that we are to protect ourselves against all the works of the devil. We increase our faith when we are equipped with the other forms of God's weapons. When we have on the breastplate of righteousness, the belt of truth, use our feet to carry the gospel, have on the helmet of salvation, and use the sword, the other weapons increase our faith alone. We are more confident when we have on the full armor of God. Our shield becomes bigger to protect us from the enemy. The more we read the Bible and pray, our faith increases tremendously. We are equipped to handle anything the devil fires at us. We need to add the shield of faith to our equipment list. Hebrews 11:1 says, "Now faith is being sure of what we hope for and certain of what we do not see." Wearing the armor itself is a step of faith that God is in control.

#95: The Ultimate Hard Hat

Take the helmet of salvation and the sword of the spirit,
which is the word of God.
—Ephesians 6:17

Along with our heart, the head is an area that we don't want to have damaged. A blow to the head can be catastrophic. For this reason, headgear is worn in many sports, such as football, baseball, and ice hockey, and hard hats are required at construction sites. A helmet also exists that protects us from spiritual harm, and that is the helmet of salvation. Symbolically, the helmet of salvation stands for Jesus Christ. Jesus means "salvation," and we know that Jesus is the cornerstone of the church. We also know Jesus is the head. In our thoughts and mind, Jesus gives us hope for tomorrow. He is the pure thing that we can strive for and He is the noble one. 1 Thessalonians 5:8 states, "But since we are of the day, let us be sober, having put on the breastplate of faith and love; and as a helmet: the hope of salvation." And Colossians 1:18 says, "And He is the head of the body, the church."

Jesus as our Lord and Savior is all the protection we need. When looking at a Roman soldier's gear, the helmet receives the most attention. In examining where someone's heart is, you can examine the mind. What comes out of the mouth was on the person's mind, and initially it was planted in his heart. If someone's heart is right, only things of God should be flowing out of his mouth, which are coming from his thoughts. Jesus protects our hearts and minds. We are always at spiritual warfare fighting the desires of our flesh. Psalm 140:7 states, "O God the Lord, the strength of my salvation, you have covered my head in the day of battle." As we fight the battles of life, we are covered by Christ Jesus. As long as Jesus is our helmet of salvation, we are protected for now and evermore. Because Jesus is the head of our body, we should strive to be more like Him. We should pattern our mind, thoughts, and actions like the Savior. Ephesians 4:14-16 says, "We should no longer be children, tossed to and fro and carried about with every wind of doctrine, by the trickery of men, in the cunning craftiness of deceitful plotting, but, speaking the truth in love, may grow in all things into Him who is the head—Christ—from whom the whole body, joined and knit together by what every joint supplies, according to the effective working by which every part does its share, causes growth of the body for the edifying of itself in love." We need to put on the helmet of salvation, and take our stand against the enemy. We will no longer let the devil deceive our minds with the cares of this world. We have the eternal hard hat.

#96: The Ultimate Weapons—The Sword and Prayer

Take the helmet of salvation and the sword of the Spirit, which is the word of God. And pray in the Spirit on all occasions with all kinds of prayers and requests. With this in mind, be alert and always keep on praying for the saints.
—Ephesians 6:17-18

Many sports use a piece of equipment that is metaphorically comparable to a sword—for example, baseball, golf, tennis, field hockey, lacrosse, and, of course, fencing. In earlier war times, the sword was a major weapon used to fight battles. But even a sword can't always guarantee a person success. We can look at how King David killed Goliath with stones, and later cut off his head with his own sword. In Ephesians 6:17, God instructs us to take up the sword of the Spirit. Symbolically, the sword represents the word of God. We need the entire sword in order to do battle with our number one opponent, the devil. When the devil attacks our finances, our relationships, and our homes, we need to fight back with the word of God. Hebrews 4:12 states, "For the word of God is living and powerful, and sharper than any two-edged sword, piercing even to the division of soul and spirit, and of joints and marrow, and is a discerner of the thoughts and intents of the heart." The biggest defense that we have against the devil is the word of God. The great thing is that the word of God serves as offense as well. When the devil or any enemy is attacking us, we can speak the word of God and back the devil up. In the same note, we can put the devil on the run by reading the word, and speaking against the devil. Therefore, out of all the weapons, the sword serves as a weapon to be used on the offense and on the defense. This concept is confirmed in Isaiah 49:2, which says, "And He has made my mouth like a sharp sword; in the shadow of His hand He has hidden me, and made me a polished shaft; In His quiver He has hidden me."

Another way to protect our armor and our bodies is through constant and daily prayer with God. We have learned that we need to put on the full armor of God in order to fight the ways of the devil. Prayer gets us in close communication with God, and God knows the battles that we are fighting. God is pleased when we go to Him in prayer, and He shows mercy and forgives our shortcomings. Prayer connects us with the spiritual battle that is going on behind the scenes. Nothing else compares with the Lord's Prayer in time of prayer and time of need. We find it in Matthew 6:9-13, which says, "Our father in heaven, hallowed be your name. Your kingdom come, your will be done, on earth as it is in heaven. Give us this day our daily bread. And forgive us our debts, as we forgive our debtors. And do not lead us into temptation, but deliver us from the evil one. For yours is the kingdom and the power and the glory forever. Amen." Reading the word and going to the Lord in prayer makes all of the other weapons more purposeful. The enemy has already been defeated. We just have to keep our shield of faith up, and we must continue to pray and read the word so we can encourage others to get on the front line.

15

Physical Obedience

#97: Obey God With Your Body

*Then Judah took a wife for Er his firstborn, and her name was
Tamar. But Er, Judah's firstborn, was wicked in the sight of the Lord,
and the Lord killed him. And Judah said to Onan, "Go in to your
brother's wife and marry her, and raise up an heir to your brother."
But Onan knew that the heir would not be his; and it came to pass,
when he went in to his brother's wife, that he emitted on the
ground, lest he should give an heir to his brother. And the thing
which he did displeased the Lord; therefore He killed him also.*
—Genesis 38:6-10

It is hard to sugar-coat this message. One of the biggest challenges that I have seen athletes and others struggle with is sexual temptation. These bodies are not ours—they are on lease from God. We are not to just please the flesh when we want to. The right way is through marriage, where people can have sexual relations with their spouse. Any sexual activity before marriage is unacceptable in God's eyes. Just gazing upon another with desiring eyes is an act of adultery. Matthew 5:27-28 states, "You have heard that it was said to those of old, 'You shall not commit adultery.' But I say to you that whoever looks at a woman to lust for her has already committed adultery with her in his heart." We must first control our eyes, because our eyes are the windows to our heart and mind. If our eyes are corrupted with sin, then our hearts and minds will absorb what's coming through the lenses of life.

In Genesis 38, we see some of the earlier days of disobedience and disrespect to women and to God. The one son Er was wicked in God's eyes, so God killed him. The Bible does not specify what Er did, but it was displeasing to the Lord. The other Brother Onan was asked to marry Tamar, his brother's wife. You would think that He would have learned from His brother's actions, but He too sinned in God's eyes. Onan was asked to produce children through his brother's wife Tamar. But during sexual relations, Onan spilled himself on the ground. Basically, he was trying not to get her pregnant. The Bible tells us to be fruitful and multiply, but God approves of that only through marriage. What Onan did was very displeasing to God as well, so God killed him too. Both brothers died because in some manner they disrespected a woman, and they also disrespected God.

We can learn from Er and Onan. We can learn that we must obey God's commands and His words. Genesis 1:28 says, "Then God blessed them, and God said to them, 'Be fruitful and multiply; fill the earth and subdue it; have dominion over the birds of the air, and over every living thing that moves on the earth.'" Onan, like many people today, wanted to please the physical desires of the flesh, and did not want to follow God's commands. How is today's world like Onan? If two people are living together before marriage, it is the same situation as Onan and Tamar. We need to ask God to examine where we are in the use of our physical bodies. Adam and Eve had some of the same temptations when plucking the apple from the tree. They were being disobedient. We need to examine how we can better serve the Lord with our bodies and actions. What do we need to give up to be right with God? God sees everything and we do serve a forgiving and merciful God.

#98: Hurting People Hurt Other People

And it was told to Tamar, saying, "Look, your father-in-law is going up to Timnah to shear his sheep." So she took off her widow's garments, covered herself with a veil and wrapped herself, and sat in an open place, which was on the way to Timnah; for she saw that Shelah was grown, and she was not given to him as a wife. When Judah saw her, he thought she was a harlot, because she had covered her face. Then he turned to her by the way, and said, "Please let me come in to you;" for he did not know that she was his daughter-in-law. So she said, "What will you give me, that you may come in to me?" And he said, "I will send a young goat from the flock." So she said, "Will you give me a pledge till you send it?" Then he said, "What pledge shall I give you?" So she said, "Your signet and cord, and your staff that is in your hand." Then he gave them to her, and went in to her, and she conceived by him. So she arose and went away, and laid aside her veil and put on the garments of her widowhood.
—Genesis 38:13-19

Like daytime soap operas, the Bible is full of adultery and romance. The Holy Bible teaches us to watch out for the drama when it comes, and to hang on to every bit of the living word of God.

The previous lesson told the story of Tamar, Er, and Onan. After God killed her first two husbands for being disobedient, Tamar was promised the younger brother Shelah in marriage, after he grew up. Tamar, who had experienced relationships with both Er and Onan probably felt lonely and rejected. She had no kids and like many others, she became impatient. The Bible really does not talk about her financial state, but she dressed up as a prostitute, and ended up having an affair with her father-in-law, Judah, which was one of the earlier forms of prostitution in the Bible.

Er and Onan somewhat turned Tamar to the streets. They were wicked in the face of God, and Tamar married both of these men. Perhaps some of their wickedness rubbed off on her. She ended up serving as a prostitute in the streets, and she even enticed her own father-in-law to produce a child. Tamar may have been having financial difficulty as well, but her actions do not line up with God's will. In this situation, we can see how wickedness can be transferred from one person to the other. Judah's actions were inexcusable as well. He slept with a prostitute, not knowing that it was his daughter-in-law. She became pregnant and had twins, Perez and Zerah. Her offspring were in the bloodline of Jesus Christ. Romans 8:28 tells us that all things are done for the good of God. We need to honor God with our bodies. We see from the Bible story of Er, Onan, Judah, and Tamar that inappropriate sexual relations can lead to death and adultery.

#99: Finding a Way Out of Temptation

Flee sexual immorality. Every sin that a man does is outside the body, but he who commits sexual immorality sins against his own body. Or do you not know that your body is the temple of the Holy Spirit who is in you, whom you have from God, and you are not your own? For you were bought at a price; therefore glorify God in your body and in your spirit, which are God's.
—1 Corinthians 6:18-19

All sin is premeditated unless a person is an unbeliever and he is not aware that he is doing wrong in God's eyes. Consequences to sin always exist, and it may be months to years before they actually show up. We all are made of dirt and clay, and we all have a flesh or sin nature. The one area that the devil attacks is the body. Our body has natural hormones that can be escalated, and it is during these temptations that we have to be strong whether married or not married. No one is exempt from sexual immorality. God makes it very clear in 1 Corinthians 6:18, and He tells us to flee from sexual immorality.

A way of escape is always possible. A person has to make up in his mind ahead of time how far a date or relationship will go. Many people go into a situation with no armor on, and they actually want to gratify the flesh. 1 Corinthians 10:12-13 states, "Therefore let him who thinks he stands take heed lest he fall. No temptation has overtaken you except such as is common to man; but God is faithful, who will not allow you to be tempted beyond what you are able, but with the temptation will also make the way of escape, that you may be able to bear it."

We all face the same temptations. The devil took Jesus to some high places, and he tempted Him several times. He attacked Jesus where He was weak. Jesus had been fasting for 40 days and 40 nights, so the devil tempted him to turn the stones into bread to satisfy his hunger. Jesus was strong and did not give in to the devil. In the same manner, we have to find ways to escape the devil, especially in the area of sexual temptation. This area has destroyed more relationships and caused more broken homes and divorces than any other area of attack by the devil. The devil knows that marriage is a covenant and a promise to God, and if he can tear it down, then he gets little victories. God always has a way of escape. We have to do our part and be prayed up in God's words, so we can make logical decisions.

When Jesus was being tempted by the devil, He used scripture and stayed on the offense. We have to be the same way. We have to use our armor, and we have to resist the devil with all our heart, mind, and soul. James 4:7-8 says, "Therefore, submit to God. Resist the devil and he will flee from you. Draw near to God and He will draw near to you." This scripture is powerful, and lets us know that when the devil comes and we resist him long enough he will flee. God also lets us know that as long as we draw near to Him, He will draw closer to us. Psalm 4:4 says, "Be angry, and do not sin. Meditate within your heart on your bed and be still."

Kings like David and his son Solomon were humbled through sexual sin. The key is to have a plan of action ahead of time. We must ask God to give us strength during times of temptation. Sometimes, it is best to be still and wait on God. Psalm 46:10 says, "Be still, and know that I am God; I will be exalted among the nations, I will be exalted in the earth."

#100: The Transformer

*I beseech you therefore, brethren, by the mercies of God, that you
present your bodies a living sacrifice, holy, acceptable to God, which
is your reasonable service. And do not be conformed to this world,
but be transformed by the renewing of your mind, that you may
prove what is that good and acceptable and perfect will of God.*
—Romans 12:1-2

Anytime we make a sacrifice, it means giving up something that we once were attached to or enjoyed in our human nature or, as the Bible sometimes refers to it, "the flesh." If we are trying to lose weight, we may have to give up certain foods that we enjoy. If the situation is saving money, it requires the discipline of not spending. Sometimes, we have to give up certain relationships that are pulling us away from our goals, and, more importantly, the relationship may be pulling us away from God. Perhaps we are too committed to our jobs and spend more time at work than we do with God and family. In order to have a serious relationship with God, it is going to cost something. It may mean breaking a lifetime habit, but in the end it will be pleasing to God.

In Romans 12:1 Paul is urging us to present our bodies as a living sacrifice. We should think about Hannah, who was without a child for a long time. She finally gave birth to Samuel, and she gave the child back to God. Samuel had a life dedicated to the priesthood, which is a major sacrifice and trusting God. Hannah waited all her life to have a child, and when she did, she made a huge sacrifice. But when you think about it, it is all God's anyway. It takes faith to give up something you have been waiting a lifetime for and trust that God will do it again. We know that a sacrifice is usually a burnt offering given to the Lord, and it is put on the altar, slain, and sacrificed to God. When we come to know Jesus Christ as our Lord and Savior, we are doing the same thing. We are saying, "Lord, I now am going to follow and trust you." We are supposed to put old ways away. We literally have to sacrifice our bodies, and turn away from old habits. We can also remember Abraham, who was willing to sacrifice his living son at the altar to obey God. God saw that Abraham was faithful to a point that he was willing to give up his only son for the Lord. God made the greatest sacrifice by releasing His only begotten Son, Jesus Christ, to us. Jesus followed through for our eternal salvation by dying on the cross for us, which is the ultimate living sacrifice, because he laid down His life for us while we were still sinners.

Once the decision of sacrifice has been made, a transformation should take place. A change of the heart should occur for the good of God. We should no longer be conformed to this world. The world thinks in this manner: I need it now; I will make that change later; nobody knows, so I can keep doing this, etc. We know that man sees the outer appearance, but God sees our heart. Being transformed means thinking like Jesus Christ, and lining up our lives the same way Jesus lived. When God made the earth, He said that it was good. Romans 8:28 says that all things are done for the good of God. God is calling us to make a renewed commitment and to conform to His will—not our will be done. We need to throw off all the things that may be hindering our walk with God, and run a good race.

#101: The Ultimate Weightwatchers

But Daniel resolved not to defile himself with the royal food and wine, and he asked the chief official for permission not to defile himself this way. Now God had caused the official to show favor and sympathy to Daniel, but the official told Daniel, "I am afraid of my lord the king, who has assigned your food and drink. Why should he see you looking worse than the other young men your age? The king would then have my head because of you." Daniel then said to the guard whom the chief official had appointed over Daniel, Hannaniah, Mishael, and Azariah, "Please test your servants for ten days: Give us nothing but vegetables to eat and water to drink. Then compare our appearance with that of the young men who eat the royal food, and treat your servants in accordance with what you see." So he agreed to this and tested them for ten days. At the end of the ten days, they looked healthier and better nourished than any of the young men who ate the royal food.
—Daniel 1:8-13

I spent many years in bodybuilding competition, and sometimes it would take six months to a year to get into the shape that I desired in order to be competitive. The larger the show or competition, the more months I needed to prepare. A national or world competition took nine months to a year to prepare for. We really are what we eat. The moment that I made the commitment to compete, I watched a transformation of my body and my mind. I would not eat certain foods during that time period, and I had a commitment to the training. God is definitely showing us in Daniel 1:8-13 that fruit, vegetables, and water are beneficial to the body. It helps the physical appearance, which helps the mind and body. God is clearly laying a pattern of how we should eat.

In Romans 12:1-3, Paul taught us not to be conformed to this world, but to transform our minds. When it comes to eating, a fast food restaurant can be found on every block in a commercial city. It is easy these days to eat on the go, because we are so busy. Daniel made a commitment that he was not going to eat the king's food. God granted him the wisdom to convince the guard to give him and his colleagues fruit and vegetables instead of royal food, which included wine. However, the understanding is deeper. The food from the king's table had not had its first portions removed, and it was ceremonially unclean. The royal food of the king was considered to be contaminated also because the first portion was offered to idols. When they made sacrifices, they made them with unclean animals, and they failed to give God their first fruits.

Daniel convinced the guard that by eating fruits and vegetables, his men would look better in 10 days and they did. What are we to learn from this story? We need to give God our first fruits, and we should not eat of the royal food. We should give God a portion of our best fruits and earnings. In the story of Abel and Cain in Genesis, we see how Cain sinned because he did not sacrifice his first fruits. We, as well, should make sure that we are giving to God what is His. Of course, we need to eat better, but the take-home message here is that we need to eat more of what God would have us to eat. Also, we need to give our first fruits to God, and we should not eat like the world eats. We must not be eating food that should be sacrificed to God.

Bonus: Where Does My Strength Cometh From?

*I know what it is to be in need, and I know what it is to have
plenty. I have learned the secret of being content in any and every
situation, whether well fed or hungry, whether living in plenty or in
want. I can do everything through Him who gives me strength.*
—Philippians 4:12-13

We rarely look under the hood of our car unless it fails to start. Rarely do we give God credit for all the oxygen we breathe. God is allowing my heart to beat as I write this book, and he is also giving me a sound mind to put words together. For some believers, it is only when an injury occurs or their health fails that they look to God for help. Our bodies are not our bodies. Our bodies belong to God who created every living thing. As stated in 1 Corinthians 6:19, our bodies are the temple of God.

The verse in Philippians 4:13 is one of the most popular scriptures in the Bible. However, many people use this verse out of context. Some people say, "I can do all things through Christ who strengthens me," but are they using God for selfish gain? This verse is true as long as whatever the request, the thing that we are trying to do is God's will and purpose for our life.

Moses doubted his ability to speak to the people and to the king. God gave Moses the words to say, and He allowed Moses to bring the people up out of Egypt. God called Moses to do the extraordinary. How do we know when we are called by God? It will be in our heart. We may run from it, and we know we are supposed to do it. However, we will not rest until God's purpose is fulfilled. Athletes and coaches often say that they can do all things through Christ who strengthens them. They think that by putting God in the equation, it will guarantee them success in becoming a pro athlete or an elite coach or in obtaining an extrinsic reward. The best thing to do is to make sure our desires line up with God, and take them to God in prayer and be patient.

We can do all things through Christ when we are following in His footsteps and when it is for Christ's gain and not self-gain. All other things added are from the grace of God. Everyone must find out what they were born to do, and when they find it, they can do all things through Christ who strengthens them. How do people find out what it is that they are born to do? First, it requires intense reading and studying of the word of God. Next, they must pay attention to what they are good at. My first swing in Little League was a homerun. At that moment, I knew that I was cut out for baseball. Ten years later, I easily walked onto the Virginia Tech baseball team. God puts the desires in our hearts, and He already knows what He has weaved us out to do. We need to think about what we can do better than most of the people in our circle, classroom, or on the job.

We can do all things through Christ who strengthens us as long as we are using the strength He has given us to bless the kingdom. Psalm 37:4 says that God will give us the desires of our heart. God is an awesome God. The next time we say that we can do all things through Him, we know that it has to be all things that are in God's will and purpose for our life.

Bonus: Disciplining the Body

Do you know that those who run in a race all run, but one receives the prize? Run in such a way that you may obtain it. And everyone who competes for the prize is temperate in all things. Now they do it to obtain a perishable crown, but we for an imperishable crown. Therefore, I run thus: not with uncertainty. Thus I fight: not as one who beats the air. But I discipline my body and bring it unto subjection, lest, when I have preached to others, I myself should become disqualified.
—1 Corinthians 9:24-27

When you watch a marathon, it starts out with hundreds and sometimes thousands of people. Only one woman and one man can win the first place prize or title. A lot of anticipation exists in a championship boxing match, and then finally a winner is crowned. In many sporting events, the number 1 team is put up against the number 2 team, which builds a lot of excitement. Someone has to win, and someone has to lose. Shortly after a championship win, the administrators and promoters are already looking ahead for the next fight or next season, which is how things go here on the earth. Everything is temporary, and very little time exists to enjoy a great victory.

A place does exist where we can have victory forever, which is in our belief of Jesus Christ. Jesus won the biggest battle and most challenging fight of all time, because He defeated the worst enemy, the devil. The devil has no power against us, because Jesus defeated the devil a long time ago when he rose on the third day from being crucified on the cross. This prize is the one that we want. It is the eternal prize, which will get our names in the book of life. 1 Corinthians 9:24 is telling us that earthly battles won are temporary. Everyone is competing to receive worldly gains, such as money, fame, houses, titles, etc. But Jesus tells us to run in a way to receive an imperishable crown. The imperishable crown does not judge whether we came in first place or last place, it looks at where our heart is in our relationship with Jesus Christ.

It is easy to speak with our lips to prove our relationship with Christ, but it is challenging to do so with our actions. The devil will fight us until the last second. 1 Corinthians 9:24-27 tells us not to waste our punches or beat at the air. When we live as the world does in trying to obtain material possession or status, we are wasting our punches. All of this stuff is temporary. We have to discipline our body daily. We have to kill our flesh daily, and renew our minds through reading of the word. Ephesians 6:13 tells us that we must escape the traps of the enemy, and we must put on the whole armor of God.

Many ballgames have been lost in the last second or final minutes. Sometimes, players let their guard down right at the end or runners let up at the finish line. When we are in this thing for Jesus, we can't let up or ever give in to the devil. The devil is always looking for a way to defeat us. He wants us to get caught in sin. The last part of 1 Corinthians 9:24-27 states, "But I discipline my body and bring it unto subjection, lest, when I have preached to others, I myself should become disqualified." We have the victory. We just have to hold on and fight until the very end. We have to ward off all temptations, and stay committed to works that Jesus Christ has called us to do. If we follow Jesus' game plan, we are assured a victory. No other way to God exists, but through Jesus Christ. He is our life coach, and He is our champion.

About the Author

Dr. Rodney Gaines is an associate professor in sport management at Virginia State University, where he also serves as the head strength and conditioning coach, working with all 16 athletic teams. He is the first person to hold that position. He also started the strength and conditioning program at Norfolk State University in 2002, where he served as a professor/strength coach. Dr. Gaines felt a call to ministry, and spent two years at Liberty University as an associate professor in health sciences and kinesiology. Dr. Gaines has served as the Bible study leader for athletes at both Virginia State University and Norfolk State University.

Dr. Gaines serves as a personal training specialist for AFAA, and he speaks two weekends a month around the country certifying others to become personal trainers. Dr. Gaines also teaches an independent leadership primer, helping others to become certified for the NSCA CSCS exam or CPT exam. Dr. Gaines is a Certified Strength and Conditioning Specialist in the NSCA and is also certified by the Collegiate Strength and Conditioning Association as a Strength Coach. Dr. Gaines also holds certifications as an ACSM Health/Fitness Specialist.

Dr. Gaines has been a bodybuilding competitor for over 22 years, and has been lifting weights for 26 years. He has won many titles, including 1995 Overall Mr. Virginia, 1998 NGA Hercules Champion, 1999 WNBF Pro Mr. Universe, 2004 Fitness Mr. Olympia, 2004 National Champion, 2004 Southern Champion, 2007 USBF Memorial Champion, 2007 NPA National Champion, and 2007 Master's World Champion. Dr. Gaines is currently retired from the sport of bodybuilding, but holds pro cards in the WNBF, NPA, USBF, NGA, and INBA.

Dr. Gaines recommitted his life to Jesus Christ after having a bout with rheumatoid arthritis in 2002. A man died beside him in the emergency room months before, and he knew that he wanted to make some changes in his life. He made a commitment to live for God and lead others to a relationship with God through his son Jesus Christ. His mission is to raise up Christian leaders and challenge them to impact their staff and athletes with the word of God. We all will impact a million souls in this lifetime. How will we impact them? Dr. Gaines' mission is to impact a million coaches and athletes with the word of God, and to continue to promote leadership with the backing of the word of God.